Close your eyes and think for a minu[...]
passionate about and know enough t[...]
zine-making that really can't be learn[...]
technique better than technique gets[...]
also know the difference. Stick to your passions and people will notice.

Zines can contain anything: comics, fiction, poetry, crafting, sex and health, cooking and food, spirituality and religion, or personal diary rants. Anything that strikes a would-be zinester as a good topic for a zine, by definition, is. Zines have existed in virtually every imaginable format, from a letter in an envelope like *Sister White* to a 60-page booklet like *Power of a Question*, where every page has some sort of three-dimensional, interactive element, to a 256-page paperback book like *We Ain't Got No Car*. The only limitation is your imagination.

The majority of zines are typed, handwritten, or computer-printed, then cut up and pasted, photocopied, and stapled into booklets. Some longer zines are taken to a print shop and printed on newsprint or bound like books. Most zines are written, designed, and constructed by one person, but certainly they can have multiple contributors and still be considered zines; literary zines or music zines featuring CD reviews often have more than one contributor. Some zines are more like art objects than magazines; for instance, hand-made on specialty paper or brown grocery bags, bound with twine, hand or machine sewn, fastened with metal brads, rubber bands or duct tape, and adorned with stickers, glitter, photographs, or rubber stamps. Some zines like *Trouble in Mind, Ideas in Pictures, Rice Harvester, Crude Noise,* and *Am I Mad...or has the whole world gone crazy?* have utilized screen-printed covers with photocopied insides.

There are zines like *Ker-bloom!*, typeset and printed by hand— entirely on a letterpress machine. Each issue is an original, limited edition piece of art. There is also *The Match!*—an anarchist journal printed using handset type on a letterpress and published since the 1960s! These zine makers have reclaimed the means of production— in every way—writing, designing, printing, distributing, and financing.

People who make and read zines don't fit easily into demographic groups. They include college students, teachers, home-schoolers, wingnuts with library cards, radical moms, women who identify, dress and pass as men, librarians, cartoonists, comedians, activists, organic farmers, childhood abuse survivors, dumpster divers and squatters, disillusioned middle-class working people, award-winning writers, bored teenagers, sex workers, and many others.

I've found zines to be the most satisfying way to project my thoughts, experiences, or interests to a relatively wide group of people (several hundred to several thousand). One reason is that readers will write honest, heartfelt, involved responses. (People who are incarcerated are particularly invested in reading and responding to zines.)

When I created a zine about the Puerto Rican Independence Movement, I received numerous responses from former movement members and admirers alike, as well as those who were not that familiar with the topic or had no idea that the leader was recently assassinated by the FBI. The technicalities of zine-making take a backseat to what you're trying to express, whether it's something that you need to purge from yourself by writing, or creating art that you don't have another outlet for, or information that you feel needs to be broadcast. When I had a vasectomy performed and created a zine about it, I was able to share the experience with plenty of individuals who were peripherally interested; many even wrote to tell me about their own vasectomy experiences.

Some zines are collected into books or developed into novels. It's important to remember that this is not necessarily the end goal. A zine is its own final product and it does not need to become a book in order to be considered valid art.

Creating zines is a way of publishing that avoids the problems of working in an increasingly stringent and impenetrable mainstream. Zines can express minority opinions, and offer space for those who aren't professional writers or artists to write and produce art. Zinesters are producing work for an established and growing readership, consisting mostly of other zinesters. Instead of producing work for a mainstream or undetermined audience, zinesters produce work for their own ever-growing community.

As Vikki Law says of her zine *Tenacious*, "in the zine community, people will read a zine about issues like the problems of women in prisons, that normally would not appear on their radar or be encountered in other media."

Because we produce our work outside of the publishing mainstream, zinesters use alternative distribution channels as well. Zines are distributed through top secret bedroom distros and sent through the mail in decorated envelopes. While personal writing abounds on blogs and websites, print zines are still thriving, and some old-school zinesters make use of new technologies to sell and promote their work. Networking sites like livejournal.com and myspace.com allow zinesters to meet lots of people doing the same thing. Fall of Autumn (www.fallofautumn.com) produces podcasts of zine writers reading their work. They've also created a wiki (an open-source online encyclopedia) at zinewiki.com.

Criticism and feedback are one of the strongest elements of community and growth in the zine world. Your peers are invested in such a manner that they want to create a current that raises all boats. As Gillian Beck says in the documentary film *$100 and a T-shirt,* "Zines are one of the only mediums where people care enough to give feedback and criticize your work" and it's because you are all part of the same community, with similar, though unstated goals.

Enough philosophy. For the purposes of this discussion, we'll assume the simplest set of circumstances: You're just starting out as a zine's single author/editor, and you want to put your thoughts and ideas on paper. Let's go!

* *Zine is spelled without an apostrophe because it has become its own word. The mainstream media often use an apostrophe, denoting that zine is not actually its own word in their eyes.*

Make a Zine!
When Words and Graphics Collide

Bill Brent & Joe Biel

with help from Sparky Taylor, Katie Haegele, Matt Holdaway,
Fly, Eleanor Whitney, Stephen Duncombe & Paul T. Olson

ISBN #978-1-934620-06-9
This is Microcosm #76068

Cover designed by MATT GAUCK & JOE BIEL
Edited by SPARKY TAYLOR
Designed by JOE BIEL

Originally published 1997 by Black Books
Second edition of 5,000 copies - Dec 1, 2008

Distributed in the booktrade by AK PRESS
sales@akpress.org
(510)208-1700

Printed in Canada at Lebonfon

Microcosm Publishing
222 S Rogers St.
Bloomington, IN 47404
www.microcosmpublishing.com

(812)323-7395

illustrations

Matt Gauck drew the beautiful cover as well as the illustrations on pages 12 and 158. He makes the zine Next Stop Adventure.

Sparky Taylor, in addition to endlessly proofing and editing the book, drew the octopus on page 7, as well as numerous other illustrations of markers, scissors, giraffes, and excited zinesters on such pages as 11, 43, 60, 80, 91, 99, 113, 121, 125, 126, 132, 137, and 141. More importantly, she helped achieve my vision for this book in every way.

David Dean is a funny and swell man who draws charming bears on pages 1-3, 6, 79, 118, 122, and 157. He plays solo music but should also make zines. He lives in Tulsa, Oklahome.

Nate Powell has a very strict breakfast routine, and ambushing him there is the only way to contact him. He did the illustrations on pages 63 and 156. His current books include Wreckage, Sounds of Your Name, and Swallow Me Whole.

Alec Longstreth has inspired many of my friends to draw and he works like Stephen King, 9-5 daily. He did the drawering on page 20 and does a comic called Phase 7.

In 2004 Mike Taylor gave me the best walking tour of Providence, RI. He makes zines like Scenery and Late Era Clash and drew the picture on page 23.

Ethan Clarke has a single argyle sock tattoo. He did a zine called Chihuahua and Pitbull and the books Chainbreaker and Leaning With Intent to Fall. He did the picture on page 38.

Erin Tobey reads more fantasy and science fiction books than anything else. She makes the zine Here It Is and did the illustration on page 42.

Bill Brown is perhaps the friendliest person I have ever met. He lives somewhere new everytime I talk to him. He does the zine Dreamwhip and drew the illo on page 54.

John Meijas got a second job as a baker to keep the price of his zine down. What's cooler than that? He does the zine Paping and did the picture on page 77.

Ben Snakepit told me that he was DIY because he catches his own fish. He does the zine Snakepit and drew the illustration on page 81.

Keith Rosson is one of my favorite punk rock philosophers who sticks around and cares. He does the zine Avow and Best of Intentions and the drawing on page 86.

Steve Larder has a funny way of communicating through his illustrations. He makes the zine Rum Lad and did the cryptic illustration on page 88.

Julia Wertz comes to me when she needs to settle a bet. I feel like she must be constantly writing new jokes. She makes the zine Fart Party and drew page 97.

Fly has been extremely supportive since I met her and has a genuine youthful excitement and energy. She does the zine Peops and Dog Dayz plus the comix chapter and page 104 illo.

Andy Singer draws the kinds of cartoons that I would, if I could draw. He does his own zine No Exit and a book of the same name plus Cartoons and drew page 109.

Nate Beaty used to host mix-tape making parties. He once suffered through me asking who sang the song Alison everytime it came on (Elvis Costello). He hangs out on a computer all day so he drew one on page 114. He makes a zine and book called Brainfag.

John Porcellino will likely never get as many props as he deserves. He practically invented the self-published comics genre with his King Cat and drew page 116.

Shawn Granton loves burritos, riding his bike, and talking about history. I mean, lots of people do, but not like this guy. He writes Ten Foot Rule and Zinester's Guide to Portland and drew page 119.

Clyde Peterson is confoundingly cool between managing the band Earth, making animation music videos, playing his own music, and making the zine In My Room. He drew 138.

Ramsey Beyer writes a zine called List so the joke was that she drew the Appendices page on 140.

Robyn Chapman is the only person I know who manages a cartooning school. She makes zines like Matching Jackets and Sourpuss but also drew 150.

Ashley Rowe is a vegan that doesn't like vegetables. We once tried to figure out how to outsmart a TV show trying to profile her. She makes Barefoot in the Kitchen and drew 145.

Greig Means is a thoughtful librarian and basketball lover. He makes the zine Clutch and did the illustration on page 16.

Eleanor Whitney is still one of my best friends even though we rarely talk anymore. I think she would win the award for "most promising future". She drew page 54.

Adam Gnade is a former newspaper editor, songwriter, future superstar, and most importantly has a sense of humor. He drew pages 7, 17, 25, 85, 87, 102, 132, and 160.

contents

One. Produce text! It doesn't matter whether you handwrite your words, type them, or cut-and-paste ransom-note style. Virtually anything is acceptable and that is the beauty of zines.

> ACTION ITEM! Zine aesthetics vary widely, in style, professionalism, and quality. Go to your local library and spend an afternoon browsing one or more good books on graphic design, especially for newsletters. Read a few dozen zines by other people and figure out what you like and don't like. If you like someone's ideas, reproduce a few things you like and try to create your own variants on a photocopier. This can help develop a sense of your own aesthetic preferences regarding graphic style. It can be very helpful to practice generating some design skills and art before you are putting together your finished zine. A lot of zinesters skip this step, but it's worth spending time thinking about.

Two. Find some pictures to go with your words. They can be photos, collages, line art, drawings, or anything else you can dream up. Do the best job you can to reproduce your images. (Images snagged from the Web are probably not of high enough resolution to reproduce well on paper). Some zines use very few images, which can hurt the overall readability. Breaking up the repetitiousness of words on the page will help readers enjoy your zine.

> **ACTION ITEM!** Far more people will pick up a zine with an interesting or provocative cover. If you're planning to sell your zine, visit a place that sells zines and notice which ones grab your attention. Try to figure out why.

Three. Set your price. Usually this is $1 to $5. You want to base your price on the cost of copying, including paper, stapling, and folding, postage, and perhaps something for your time (even if it's just coffee, cookies, or the occasional slice of pizza!). If there are other expenses (phone bills, a PO Box rental, envelopes, photos, etc.), plan for those as well. Most people who will sell your zine for you, like stores and distributors, will take 40-60% of the cover price. If you want to sell your zine through these channels, think about this when setting your price. Some people prefer only to sell their zines directly to their readers. Think about including the price on the cover if you are selling it in stores.

Four. Include your address. This is vital. Many people include both a postal address and an e-mail address. The best place is the inside cover or first page. Sometimes people also put it on the back cover, if they are mailing it without an envelope. The exception is if you're publishing something so subversive or illegal that you don't want it traced back to you. It is easy to be anonymous, with the way that zine distribution functions. You need to decide whether you feel comfortable printing your home address or renting a PO Box for security and privacy. Most zinesters rent a box from the Postal Service (cheapest) or from a private mail drop company (less cheap). A private mail drop may be more convenient if they have longer hours and can accept a wider range of deliveries. Some provide copying services and other conveniences. One zinester told me that he rents a private mailbox because its address resembles an apartment's, on the off chance that readers would attempt to visit. So it can be a way of tricking would-be stalkers and other creeps.

 "One of the real nice things about PO boxes is they provide a stable address for those who move, especially all who don't depart on good terms with their landlord. Even in the best cases, this happens a surprising number of times. I have many zines [which use] many different addresses for the same zine. You are supposed to tell the Postal Service whenever you change your address, but you don't have to, so this makes it a nice secure address." – Steve Kudlak, West Virginia Zine Archivist

Five. Print some copies. Unless you're blessed with deep pockets or unlimited access to free copies, it's a safe bet to make 100 or 200 copies to start. At this volume, it makes the most sense to photocopy your zine, rather than having it printed by an offset printer, web printer, print-on-demand, or other mass production method.

Unless you have an obvious place to make copies, it makes sense to call around and figure out who has the best price for the volume that you are printing. Sometimes one shop will match or beat another's price. Don't be afraid to ask for a deal, but it is more likely in smaller copy shops than national chains. The chains have business partnerships with online retailers such as Amazon, and national organizations such as Publishers Marketing Association, so they only give their sellers or members a discount on copying and related services. Befriending the staff is very helpful, as it'll make your relations much more pleasant – and sometimes grant you special pricing.

It's helpful to ask around for references or print samples of similar work. Figure out a firm schedule with your printer and stick to it. Treat the printer with respect; a good shop is an invaluable source of information on how to adjust the size of your zine, page count, or colors to get the lowest price. The more controversial your material is, the more important it is to have a strong, personal relationship with your printer. We have horror stories of trying to get sexually-oriented material, anti-Republican propaganda, or even zines with peculiar names printed. Conversely, there is no reason to stay with a printer who is disrespectful to you or your work.

Six. Get reviewed! Send copies of your zine to reviewers at publications like *Zine World* and the others listed in the Appendix of reviewers. It's a simple and effective way to find people interested in reading your zine and communicating with people who share your interests. Because that's what it's all about, right?

Seven. Distribute your zine. Think about who to give or sell your zine to. It could be friends, family, co-workers, or other people who make zines. These people can be reached through reviews, local stores, far away stores, and distributors ("distros"). Check out the appendices for names and addresses!

Eight. (Optional) A mailing list. Figure out a way to keep track of it. Scraps of paper in a shoebox, a notebook, a card file, an address book in an email program, or a database can all be functional, as long as you can find the information when you need it.

Making a zine is that simple. Everything else is based on these eight basic steps.

what's a zine?

Various people define this differently. A popularly agreed upon definition is *a short-run periodical produced more from passion than intention to make money.* Press runs range between ten and ten thousand copies, with the vast majority around two hundred. It is rare to start a zine with commercial motives. Those who do make money are typically not motivated by it. Any hope of a reasonable hourly wage is extremely unlikely.

Zines are one of the most immediate and disposable popular literary forms of the past two hundred years. Zines are typically less formal, and far less commercial productions than most magazines.

What most zines share is a preference for content over form. A zine is a functional vehicle for self-expression. Folks in the zine world do not view a zine as a "lesser" format. Without the fear of losing advertising revenue or offending its readership, a zine can take on topics the mainstream media ignores. Zinesters often are the first to capture events because they are closer than their glass-tower counterparts to the issues as they are happening. Music zines usually cover up-and-coming bands that would never break commercially and are unlikely to be "discovered" by big music magazines. Others report on the seamy underside of society in intimate detail. Still others focus intensely, even obsessively, on small niches of culture or society that the big guys ignore. Taken as a group, zines contain some of the most unique and subversive writing and thought available in any format today.

For instance, John Marr explores bizarre murder cases in each issue of *Murder Can Be Fun*. Eric Ruin, Meredith Stern, and Andy Cornell use their zines, *Trouble in Mind, Crude Noise,* and *Secret Files of Captain Sissy* to dissect, critique, and discuss the radical political movements that they are a part of. Lauren Martin wrote intellectual feminist and cultural analysis in her zine, *Quantify*. Dave Roche used his zine *On Subbing* to tell his daily stories of working as a substitute special education assistant in Portland's public schools. *Shark Fear, Shark Awareness* is exactly what the name suggests: An informative and reverent guide to sharks!

Why Make A Zine?
To have your work in print. To share what you can make. To encourage others creatively. To connect with folks who share your interests. To get mail. To make new friends. To create the kind of publication you've always wished existed. To teach yourself. To see your work in print by any means necessary. To communicate very passionately in a medium that is intensely personal. Whatever your interests or agendas, a zine allows you to express your opinions, art, and ideology to a wide audience in a fun, relatively cheap way.

For still others, it is an intensely personal experience that helps to deal with living in an insane world. I found a great explanation on alt.zines. Christine, who did a zine called *Post Modern Toad,* posted:

"Why Publish a Zine?"
"Actually, a LOT of people have asked me that same question... but quite not in the same context. It's more like, "Why the hell are you wasting your time with this thing?" Like I need to hear that from someone who's apparently never, EVER, had a creative idea in his entire life. <grin>
"Deep down, doing something creative, like publishing a zine, or writing a poem, or painting a landscape, is therapeutic. For me, the creative urge has always seemed to scream during the most difficult times in my life. I've learned (the hard way) to NEVER ignore that urge when I'm feeling down—unexpressed creative energy makes me feel even worse! Who needs that? Focusing that energy

on doing something positive is a hell of a lot more constructive than sitting around feeling sorry for yourself. If someone doesn't understand it, or doesn't appreciate it, or even if they totally hate it...that really doesn't matter at all. Before anyone else has even seen it, it's served its purpose—YOU'VE FINISHED IT. You've accomplished something, and it's something to be proud of. Even if you're not 100% happy with it (and who ever really is?!?), you've still created something that's at least meaningful to you. And if you've entertained someone else in the process, all the MORE power to you!"

Your first zine is more of a learning process than anything else. You make it, get feedback, learn from your mistakes, and keep getting better. If you saw the early issues of some long-running zines, you'd be shocked at how rough they were. Better to get it done than to delay by trying to make it perfect. Once you get over your fear and get that first issue in people's hands, you'll find the second one is a lot easier. Either you'll want to prove to folks it wasn't a fluke, or you'll want to show them you're capable of even better. Bottom line: the first issue is always the hardest. Just get it done and go from there.

Sometimes, especially with your first zine, you may want things to be perfect. But in five years, you might have different thoughts and opinions, and better skills at design. You'll cringe at the awful layout and groan as you read the awkward phrasing. Maybe you'll want to track down every copy and burn it. At the same time, it'll be your favorite zine ever because you did it, and that's something to be proud of.

What's So Special About Zines?
Zines are the ultimate do-it-yourself project. I've always admired initiative and, as Christine indicates above, I believe that most great zines are great because the editor felt *driven* to publish them. A great zine transcends limitations of funds, likelihood, experience, and technology.

Most zines have a short life span. One reason is that it is often hard to sustain the initial enthusiasm that created them. Family commitments, work, loss of interest, and plain old burnout get in the way, and the zine is abandoned, often leaving a trail of disappointed fans in its path.

But zines are fun while they last, both for the writer and the reader. And the definitions of "writer" and "reader" can be amazingly fluid. This is one of the most exciting things about zines. Many readers of a zine eventually became its writers, and many readers are inspired to produce their own zines. As Clem Burke, who has drummed for Blondie and the Ramones, once said about being a rock musician, "I do what I do because I was always a big fan. The ultimate fan transcends fandom and does it himself."

Zines are the ultimate expression of the do-it-yourself ethic. Thus it is to the aspiring or current zine maker that this book is dedicated.

So how do *I* make a zine?
Look at other zines and see what you like and don't like. Most importantly, you want your zine to be your own. There's not much point in blatantly copying someone else's zine. Yet there have been plenty of incidents of people taking a finished zine by someone else, putting their name and address on it, and copying it as their own. Ridiculous, right? You want to learn from others' mistakes and successes, not steal them.

Planning is easy, yet skipping this step can lead to much trouble down the line. It is important to decide what you want in a particular issue of your zine, how you want it to flow, what order it will appear in, where that material will come from, and when you need it by.

There are no set rules about this. Some people put together a zine with nothing more than a pen and never touch a keyboard. Some type on clunky, old manual typewriters, electric ones, or occasionally word processing machines with built-in printers. A few even have everything typeset professionally, from computer files, without ever creating a paper master. Beginning folks doing zines tend to type text with computers, print it out on inkjet printers, and paste it onto the page with graphics. Personally, I think this isn't the easiest way to make a zine and it can look more like a school report than a creative endeavor. Experiment and think about what would work best for you.

Start an issue with one of your strongest pieces to get people's attention right away. Don't start the issue with something that is more than a few pages long. Inserting graphics early on helps, since this also gets readers into the zine more quickly.

by Matt Holdaway

The oldest known woodcut print in the world is Darani Sutra found inside Seokga Pagoda of Bulguksa Temple, Korea printed before 751 A.D. It predated Japanese Million Pagoda Darani Sutra dated 770 A.D. Chinese printers used wood blocks with carved characters and inked paper in the 8th century. In the 11th century Pi Sheng created early moveable type, allowing for letters to be rearranged. Movable metal type was a development associated with woodblock printing, such as slow engraving. There is a record that Sangjeong-gogeum-yemun (Prescribed Ritual Texts of the Past and Present) was printed with movable type around 1234 A.D.

Johann Gutenberg invented the printing press in 1454, revolutionizing the transmission of information using metal moveable type and an ink made from turpentine, lampblack, and linseed oil. Within 50 years, over 500,000 texts had been printed (almost exclusively religious works). Besides the Bible, one of the first important uses of the Gutenberg press was to print a handbook for the Church called "Malleus Malefactorum," which outlined how to find and expose "witches." It allowed the Church to quickly distribute a kind of uniform code throughout Europe, and is the reason that inquisition questions and procedures across the continent were so quickly disseminated and so similar.

Gutenberg's invention coincided well with the Reformation. Europe, unified as "Christendom" for a millennium, was suddenly ripping apart, and one of the main reasons was that viewpoints opposed to the Vatican were being printed and distributed. Luther's 95 theses, the document that started the conflict, was an early zine – the writing wouldn't have ignited a war if it hadn't been published and passed around.

After 200 years of struggle in England, printers won the right to publish in the 1700s. Beginning around 1760, the Industrial Age created a need for educated workers, which created public schools and wider literacy. Self-publishing was too expensive for most, yet the number of books and pamphlets increased. Ben Franklin self-published as a youth. Samuel Adams, Thomas Payne, and other Americans printed works that helped bring about the American Revolution.

In England, William Blake self-published using etched copper plate engraving. Around 1850, an inexpensive small tabletop printing press, not much more than a toy, introduced "amateur journalism," a popular hobby, especially among boys. Todd Lincoln published on one from the White House, and Lloyd Osborne did a "zine" with contributions from his stepfather, Robert Louis Stevenson. The mimeograph was introduced by Edison circa 1875 and soon became standard office (and church basement) equipment. Dadaists began self-publishing writings and book art in the early 1900s.

And then it happened: In 1929, readers of science-fiction magazines started communicating via mimeographed or spirit-duplicated "fanzines." Pulp novel publishers were inundated with reader mail nitpicking technical details in their stories. So editors began printing letters – complete with full addresses. Fans began writing to each other and forming networks. This led to fanzines about topics such as horror, wrestling, and science fiction. *The Comet*, a science fiction zine composed mostly of articles on science, began publishing in 1930. Other science fiction zines followed, including *Time Traveler* and *Science Fiction*, edited by Jerome Siegel and Joe Schuster, who also created Superman. Many sci-fi zine editors still publish, though most now photocopy or publish online.

Starting in the 1950s, mimeograph technology was used to self-publish literature, including chapbooks and manifestos by the Beats.

American and British punks of the 1970s created the form closest to today's zines, seldom having heard of the original fanzines. Using clip art, they created their own media, using zines to promote independent music and clubs. Cheap and available photocopying made it easier than ever for anyone who could make a flyer to make a zine.

In 1938, Chester F. Carlson obtained the first patents for the photocopier. In 1937, he developed the process of xerography or "dry copy," a process based on electrostatic electricity. Xerography comes from the Greek term "dry writing." Over twenty companies turned down Carlson's invention, and it took him six years of demonstrating its function before the Battle Development Company took interest and produced his invention in 1944. The Haloid Company negotiated the commercial rights. Haloid became Xerox and introduced the first commercial photocopier in 1958.

In high school, Chester Carlson was a self-publisher himself, using mimeograph. Underground comix artists used the photocopier for self-publishing almost immediately following its introduction. *Rolling Stone* started as a zine. Sergei Kovalev, Tatyana Khodorovich, and Tatyana M. Velikanova self-published *The Chronicle of Current Events* in Russia. Many Russian self-publishers attempted to create a "close circle of like-minded people who spoke their own language, inconceivable to others" under threat of lethal persecution. Even though dissent was not the primary object of many self-publishers, Velikanova was arrested for printing her views, spending four years in a prison camp and five years in exile.

In contrast, a number of people in the USSR self-published purely for dissent, spreading views against nuclear arms and their government's oppression. While not as severe, Americans in the 1960s faced persecution for publishing their work, such as Alan Ginsberg's poem *Howl*. Ginsberg was subjected to a long court trial in which poets and professors were summoned to "prove" that *Howl* was not obscene.

Factsheet Five documented the zine explosion of the 1980s. The original editor, Mike Gunderloy, a pillar of the science fiction fanzine community, popularized the word "zine" and established most of today's "zine ethos" (non-profit, trading, DIY, importance of feedback from readers, etc.) based on his background in the science fiction fanzine tradition.

Technological advances in the 1990s made professional editing and publishing tools accessible to the general public. Mainstream media became interested in zines that had for the most part remained in obscurity for years. They tended to view zines as a novelty rather than as a legitimate form of art or literature. Retail stores began to carry zines as part of their books, comics, or music sections. By the end of the '90s, many who had published popular zines for years stopped publishing, moved into more mainstream creative endeavors, or began to devote their time and creativity to websites.

Today, zines owe creative debts not only to the punk fanzines of the 1970s, but the riot grrl movement of the 1990s. Riot grrl zines were crafted by political feminists, harnessing years of pent-up anger and frustration in the form of cut-and-paste collage and a wicked sense of humor.

The zine explosion of the past two decades had made many people aware of zines. However, the frequent lack of quality jaded some would-be retailers and readers. Digging for the diamond in the rough became more of a challenge and time commitment.

On the other hand, the absence of many long-running zines and the lack of mainstream attention created a fresh, open environment. While mediocre zines were still created, the awareness of what had come before motivated many individuals to create book-art zines and other forms requiring extensive time and effort. Many zine publishers returned to printing methods like silkscreen, letterpress, linoleum cut, and also to hand-stitched bindings.

The use of the Web has created more extensive networks of people working within the same medium. It provides a virtual retail area, increasing reader access to remote locations, and allowing more people to see content than the self-publisher could afford to non-virtually print. Annual conventions aid and regenerate public awareness while strengthening relations among self-publishers.

Today, people who stick to print do so because of its warm, human feel, or distinctive artistic elements. You can use printing techniques that create texture, create pull-out sections, insert envelopes, insert bags with scents, use different kinds of paper, and incorporate other elements that make your zine unique and unable to be reproduced on-screen. Similarly, zines offer an intimate connection in the kinds of information they convey, the vulnerability that the authors often provide, and the simple fact that you can read them in the park, on the bus, or on the toilet.

Your zine is more likely to succeed if your space is organized. Whether your office is an actual room, the corner of a garage, or a combination of a laptop and the local copy place, you need a system for retrieving important things in a timely manner. It pays to set up this system early on. It's okay for your space to be cluttered or crowded, as long as you can find things when you need them.

Mail. If you're getting a lot of letters, orders, or submissions, you need some way to organize them, or at least keep them together until you have time to respond. Bill keeps them all in a Postal Service mail tub. Joe has a series of document sorters and folders. Maybe you'll even deal with each submission as it arrives—it is often the impossible ideal. The important thing is to keep everything in one place until it's time to deal with it.

Use a tray to organize chronologically what is owed you, and a different one for what you owe others. This way, you can tell at a glance when something is due. When a bill comes in, mark the back of the envelope with the amount to pay, and the date to pay it, factoring in enough days to allow for mail delivery.

If you work with others on your zine, make a box or tray for each person's notes. It helps everyone to stay organized and feel a part of the team.

Try to stay caught up on your mail. It is very difficult to catch up once you fall behind. Maybe a friend can occasionally deal with anything you don't have time for, but it's best to organize this from day one. If you can't keep up, it's okay sometimes to discourage any further submissions or mail.

Delegating the workload. If you start to receive lots of mail, especially orders, you'll probably need to delegate the data-entry and order-filling responsibilities, or one person will never have time to deal with writing and editing also. Creating a job description for each person working on the project is a very good idea.

Data entry. You need to decide on a method for tracking data right from the start. This can change later on, but you'll need something to record with – be it a notebook, filing cabinet, computer program, or just a pile of paper scraps in a drawer – as long as all of the information is there. It's very important to keep track of things reliably – especially orders.

If you use a computer, you have many options. As a database, FileMaker is great for keeping address lists and tracking orders, but QuickBooks is much better for finances. If you can get a dedicated accounting program to generate invoices, tell you when bills are due, balance your books, and figure out your taxes (presuming you've got enough income from your zine hobby to report them), by all means do so. Sometimes people will use programs for tasks other than their intended purposes, which can make life more difficult. Let the tool fit the job.

File cabinets and related hiding places. Hanging folders in a file cabinet work great if you have that much data to store. You may want to hold onto things like mock-ups, proofs, leftover paper from various print jobs; artwork for ads; submissions for upcoming issues; distributor paperwork, etc. It's also a good idea to have paper printouts of anything that you keep on a computer.

One of the greatest discoveries I ever made was a friend's file cabinet of zines. People who do zines always have stacks of other people's zines around. If you can afford the space, a tall, four-drawer file cabinet is the perfect way to store your zine collection. Hanging folders make great zine organizers if you can afford them. Milk crates work great too and last forever. It sure beats boxes or stacks on the floor.

A short filing cabinet (two drawers) makes a great stand for a laser printer, copier, or scanner. It can also be an emergency layout table / mail sorter / bill-paying desk. Create horizontal space in your workspace, do your best to keep it clear, and you will have an easier, more satisfying place to work.

An **in box and an out box** on top of your desk might be a sorting system that suits you. It seems to work well in movies and spoof cartoons. The good and bad news is that if you ignore something for too long, it generally ceases to be important.

An **erasable white board** or corkboard is great for making notes and leaving reminders about current projects, priorities, deliveries, and outstanding consignments.

Assembly area

You need a large area to assemble your zine, preferably one where you can leave your layout undisturbed as it develops. A cheap light table comes in handy. New ones can be pricey ($70 and up). A light table with a see-through plastic grid on it allows you to see whether you're pasting objects straight. One way to make one is to cut a sheet of thin white plastic to fit over the top of an aquarium or wooden box, into which you place a suitable light. Notch the cover in one corner so that you can run the light cord out of the box. Sometimes you can find used tables at a thrift store, rummage sale or in the classifieds. Originally I got a slightly damaged one from a friend who works in the publishing field, then bought a cheap drafting table. Finally, I inherited a friend's light table (an old Knox Acculight, the angled kind of table used for viewing slides), which I am sure will last me for the rest of my life. It even has large sliding drawers underneath, which I use to store all my craft supplies. It's all about finding or creating something that works for you.

Your **desk** will stay neater longer if you use small trays or other dividers in the drawers. Keep a can filled with pencils, pens, and a letter-opener on your desk. We got almost all our furniture as hand-me-downs from friends, thrift stores, trash, and the downsizing corporate world. There's also craigslist.org. A cheap desk is easy to find.

Throw out stuff constantly. If you haven't used it in six months, then you probably don't need it. Stuff accumulates rapidly, though most of us are slow to trash it. Every time you handle a piece of paper, question whether you really need to keep it. Pass other people's zines along when you're through with them – unless they really blow your mind and you'll want them in ten years!

And finally, **the cat sleeps on top of everything.** The more precariously balanced the stack, the more likely that the cat will send it crashing to the floor. Wade, our cat at Microcosm, takes great joy in pushing anything onto the floor, sitting between people and their computers, and stepping squarely on the escape key.

Layout and type are the most important elements to consider when designing your zine. Layout deals with the placement of elements on the printed page, as well as the overall organization of pages. The type you choose communicates a lot about your zine: its legibility, its attitude, and sometimes its budget.

This section will acquaint you with the basics of layout and type. We suggest borrowing or buying a couple of specialized books devoted to these topics. Here we start with planning and creating a mock-up of your zine, progressing through layout and type, and on to printing and finishing your publication. Much of this chapter may sound like it only applies to using a computer to produce your zine, but most of the techniques also apply to a handwritten or typewritten style.

What's involved in page planning?
Page planning is when you determine page orientation and paper size, margin and column sizes, spacing between lines and paragraphs, paragraph alignment (left, right, justified, or mixed), primary typefaces, and perhaps some fun stylistic elements such as ruling lines. (Editor's note: "nerds!")

Orientation and Size
Zines come in every size, but the most common in the US are: *half-letter* or *digest,* which is a standard 8-1/2" x 11" sheet folded in half to 5-1/2" x 8-1/2", and *standard,* which is either an 8-1/2" x 11" sheet, unfolded, or an 11" x 17"

sheet folded to 8-1/2" x 11". *Quarter* is a half-size cut into two pieces to 5-1/2" x 4-1/4", or to 4-1/4" x 5-1/2". Another size that shows up regularly is *half-legal*, which yields a 7" x 8-1/2" format. European paper sizes differ, but they are rough equivalents to the American ones. Both are shown to the right.

Making a Sketch

Drawing a rough sketch helps you to determine how much space you can allot to each piece and gives you an idea where to put graphic elements, like photos, ads, line art, and illustrations. Do a sketch for each page. The easiest way to design a page is to take a blank piece of paper and draw your document layout using lines to represent text, as shown below.

Defining the Elements

Next, define the basic document elements (paragraphs, headings, rules, typefaces, margins, columns, etc.). Will you indent your paragraphs? Which typefaces will you use for your headings and pull quotes? Will you use ruling lines for them? How much space do you want between lines of text? Some of these choices will depend on your technology, or lack thereof.

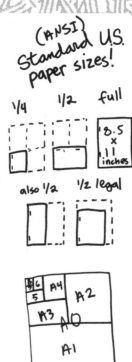

European paper size chart

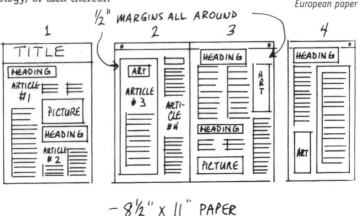

If you have a desktop publishing or word processing program, you may want to adapt one of its pre-packaged templates; try the ones for newsletters. If you modify a template, be sure to give it a new name to avoid writing over the original.

How Do I Keep Track of What Goes Where?

Most zines, booklets, and chapbooks are laid out so that each actual sheet has four pages printed on it. It's easy to see why. Fold a sheet of paper in half. Now number the resulting sides: one, two, three, and four. You have just created a mock-up of a four-page zine. You probably want to create your zine in four-page multiples, since this is the format that your photocopier or printing house is setup to deal with. Even a full-length book like the one you are reading right now ends up as a four-sheet multiple, even if there are some blank, unnumbered pages at either end.

There is one exception to the four-page-multiples rule. Some zines are not folded; they are just stapled along the edge, usually at the top, middle, and bottom. I don't like this format much, because it is flimsy and can be awkward for the reader turning pages. Often the staples pull out. There are some advantages, though: you can use a two-page multiple rather than four (such as 18 pages). Also, it can save you the trouble of folding and trimming (described below).

I recommend creating a mock-up of your entire zine with sheets of folded paper. In the professional world, this is known as a "dummy." A **dummy** *helps you visualize the zine as a whole, since you can mark on the pages what goes where and then see how it all fits together*. A dummy can also help you explain things to the printer later on. So, if you're making a 16-page zine or booklet, it's then easy to see that your layout must put pages 2 and 15 on the backs of pages 1 and 16.

a 20 page zine mock-up

HINT: To hold the dummy together, take a rubber band or paper clips and place them down the middle fold. (We've seen finished zines that used the "rubber band" method of binding, though we don't recommend this.)

In a book, you can always leave some pages blank if you are a bit short of text. Unlike books, a zine is expected to have something on every page. You may need to come up with some space-fillers such as jokes, quotes, and illustrations. I always have some ad trades (such as ads for other zines) that I can drop in when I have the room, or omit when I don't.

Try to finish editing all of your writing before you start layout. It will save you a lot of frustration. One seemingly minor addition or deletion can affect the placement of text for many pages. If you are going to include a table of contents, save it for last.

Page Numbering
Printing page numbers is a good idea. It helps readers orient themselves and goes a long way toward making your zine seem more professional. Sometimes zines include their cover in the page count. Be consistent about how you refer to page numbers, or you will confuse readers.

How Do I Make My Zine Look Good?
Placement
Professional designers often use grid paper (or computer equivalent) when drawing page layouts. Grid paper helps you draw even lines and balance your columns.

If you have one graphic element that must go on a specific page (like an ad or photo), place that first, and then build your page around it. You can vary the grid from page to page, but when you're just starting to experiment with layout, usually it's better to keep things pretty simple and consistent.

White Space
White space is any space on the pages that is blank, such as margins. Effective use of white space is important because it makes your zine easier and more appealing to read. Surrounding an item with white space usually makes it stand out. A dense and cluttered layout is often hard to read. Pages can get so crowded that they confuse readers and discourage them from continuing. Creative use of white space avoids this problem.

Columns
For your readers' sake, use at least 1/4" gaps between columns. Otherwise the

Some layout examples. Think of your options besides plain text on a page.

columns seem to run together. Readers grow tired when columns contain more than 65 letters on average. Too many narrow columns can be frustrating to read too. It's fine to vary the number of columns per page. This is a good way to set off a chart, or to draw focus to a particular item, like an important article. One common effect is to place a picture in the middle of two columns of text, with the text flowing around either side. The picture can be centered between the columns, or off-center.

Margins

Try to define page margin settings that can serve as the basis for every page in your zine. This simplifies a range of tasks such as folding and stapling. A consistent margin will also appeal to readers.

Leave at least 1/2″ blank on all four sides of your page. This reduces the risk of cutting off text or images that are close to the edge. This is especially important for offset printing, where many presses require some extra space on the edges to allow for proper rolling and trimming. Many presses require gripper space at the top of each page to hold the master as it runs through the press, so don't place your images too close to the top. Check with your printer about this.

You'd think you could just create equal margins all around your page. However, this tends to make the top margin look larger than the sides, and the bottom margin will look small. Instead, make the side margins equal, the top margin slightly smaller, and the bottom margin larger (up to twice the size of the top).

You can have separate margin settings for left and right pages if you wish. Use slightly wider margins on the inside of each page to allow plenty of space for stapling or binding. This also makes it easier to read, since the text isn't stuck in the gutter of the fold.

(Paper width) − (column widths + gutter widths) = X
X = total width for left and right margin settings.

Think of each set of facing pages as a unit rather than as two unrelated parts. You want to create a unit in which the margin between the pages is about equal to each of the outer margins. Experiment a bit with margins before making your final decision. You'll want facing pages to complement each other and have similar contrast and appearance.

Type Basics

Type is the published form of writing. The study of typefaces and how to use them is called typography. The best way to learn about type is to observe how it is used on the page. You can start by studying the newspaper, signs, and labels. Most of the origins of typesetting, kerning, leading, type size, and spacing trace back to hand-set letter press. Thus, if there is a letterpress shop in your town, I recommend visiting it. It can show you the true flexibility and decision-making involved in type spacing.

Most typefaces have at least four styles: normal, **bold,** *italic,* and ***bold italic.*** For our purposes here, those are probably the only ones you need to know about.

"I Thought They Were Called Fonts?"

Technically, a font is a specific typeface in a specific size, generally referring to a typeface on a computer. These words have become fairly interchangeable in general use. The advent of computer typefaces, with their ease of size changing, makes the traditional definition of "font" fairly obsolete.

"I Want to Use All of Them!"

If you do, your pages will probably be very distracting, and confuse and alienate your readers. Try to limit the number of typefaces on a page to two. In fact, it's not a bad idea to limit the number of typefaces in your entire publication to three or four until you become more experienced with type. Many folks can get by with one or two.

As with any rule, this one has exceptions. On your cover and in any ads you create, you can use different typefaces to set them apart from the rest of your zine. Also, if you have a number of short pieces, you can create some dramatic effects by using a different font for each heading.

This is **bold,** most often used for **headings** and for **emphasis;** This is *italic,* most often used for titles of publications, such as *The New York Times,* and creative works, such as Mozart's *Requiem* or *Gone With The Wind*. It can also be used for *emphasis;* and finally, this is ***bold italic,*** which is hardly ever used unless you want to make a ***really emphatic point. Don't use this as your text face, or you will drive your readers crazy. It's like shouting everything in a really LOUD voice.***

Here is a heading in 12-point bold.

Here is body text in 10-point book.

Here is a caption in 8-point italic.

Different size type can be used to distinguish text with different functions. Body text is usually done in 10-point type because it is a very readable size. To distinguish headings and captions from body text, vary the point size by at least two points. Thus, 8-point type can be used for captions, and 12-point type for headings. You can vary the style or weight, perhaps using bold for headings and italics for captions.

If you get seriously interested in type, you may wish to get on the mailing lists of the various type houses to receive their catalogs. Everyone from the big guys like Adobe and Monotype to the smaller fish like Emigré have something interesting to offer, and their catalogs often use type in creative ways that can inspire your own layouts. You can find their ads, as well as lots of practical information on type, in magazines like *Publish*.

To be clear, we aren't type purists. Neatly handwritten zines lend an honest, informal quality to a personal zine that the homeliest typeface can never match. If you are complimented on your cursive or block letter style, it's something to consider. Of course, there's now computer programs that can turn your handwriting into a computer font, so we've come full circle.

Typographic Hints!
- Mixing handwriting and typing can look neat if you do it right. Perhaps handwrite your titles while typing the articles, or vice versa.
- It's hard to make titles and headings too big. You can use a different typeface than the one you choose for body text. Bold, thick typestyles work well. You can also use white text reversed on a black box (which you can create with the inverse feature on some photocopiers). This will add visual variety right off the bat while helping the reader organize your article, particularly a long one, into more digestible visual pieces.
- Set your body text large enough to read easily. Photocopying, in particular, can lower the quality. It often blurs the text slightly, which can make small text hard to read. Try not to set any type smaller than 8 points. If you are printing from a computer, be sure to use the high-resolution mode set to 600 DPI or the "best quality" setting.
- There are two basic types of fonts:
This is a sans font. This is a serif font.
     - Serif characters have little twigs and loops ("serifs") hanging off the lines, whereas sans serif (French for "without serifs") type does not. Supposedly these "connectors" make type easier to read. Serif fonts are easier to read for larger font sizes, particularly in long blocks of text.
- Sans serif is commonly used in smaller text, headers and footers, signs, and pull quotes.

If you are using larger text, it is usually best for short bursts of text and titles.

- Vary type size and style for emphasis. Avoid using underlining when it's not appropriate. Bold or italic type tends to look better.

- Avoid widows and orphans (one line of text by itself at the top or bottom of a page respectively). Avoid putting titles at the bottom of a page. Follow headings with at least two lines of text before a page break.

- Do not use all uppercase letters for body text, and only in short bursts for titles. It can be difficult to read. All lowercase letters can be distracting but can also create a specific style and feel.

- Learn to use drop caps (an oversize letter, usually a capital) to start articles and section headings. This is a useful visual variety technique. They look great in pull quotes, too. Drop caps can be tricky at first, but they're worth the time to make things look interesting.

- Keep most sentences short, preferably no longer than 12 words each.

- It is usually easier to read text in two or three columns than across the full width of a page, unless your zine is very small.

- Be careful when wrapping text around an image, as it is nearly impossible to follow where to read and disrupts any natural habit that the brain has for reading across the page. Layout programs can mechanically do this, but they can't help you make the judgment decisions of what looks good or not.

- Consider placing images at the side, top, or bottom of the page or between two text columns to avoid breaking up a line of text.

DO THIS:

ZINES

Zines are swell and fabulous. We love zines more than life itself. A day without zines is like a day without sunshine. Q: How many zine editors does it take to change a light bulb? A: None, they'll just edit in the dark until someone else can afford to buy the light bulb. Zines are cool, zines are fine, we like zines all the time. Hooray for zines!

NOT THIS:

ZINES

Zines are swell and fabulous. We love zines more than life itself. A day without zines is like a day without sunshine. Q: How many zine editors does it take to change a light bulb? A: None, they'll just edit in the dark until someone else can afford to buy the light bulb. Zines are cool, zines are fine, we like zines all the time. Hooray for zines!

Hyphenation.
If you are using layout software, you can spend more time fixing bad auto-hyphenation than inserting hyphens manually. Turn it off and customize to your liking. Don't hyphenate less than three letters at the end of a line, or more than two consecutive lines. If you are concerned, break words between syllables. *Eliminate word breaks across pages*. It breaks the reader's concentration.

Justification.
Justified text can look lousy. Avoid justifying narrow columns, or you'll run into a lot of problems with weird spacing t   h   a   t l o o k s s t r e t c h e d – o u t. Weird hyphenations abound in justified text, so everything from the previous paragraph goes double here. Centered headings look better across justified columns. Unless you really like the justified look, I suggest using left-justified (sometimes called "ragged right") headings and text.

Drawing Focus: Pull quotes, Reverse Text, and More
There are many ways to draw focus to particular elements on your page. I've mentioned surrounding an item with white space, but there are a lot of others. Judicious use of these methods will help avoid the "gray page" syndrome that results when your zine is nothing but similar lines of type.

HINT: Blur your sight slightly by narrowing or widening your eyes. Now look at your page. What jumps out? Is it just a wash of gray with no variety? Use this trick throughout the layout stage as a way to check the appearance of your pages. You can try it in front of a rack of magazines to improve your cover design too.

A pull quote is a popular magazine trick, which involves pulling out an attention-getting or summarizing phrase in an article, and repeating the phrase in enlarged type, spanning it across one or more columns.

A pull quote is a popular magazine trick, which involves pulling out an attention-getting or summarizing phrase in an article, and repeating the phrase in enlarged type, spanning it across one or more columns. Often these have a *drop cap* (a big capital) as the first letter. Pull quotes serve to draw a reader's attention to a particular point, and they really break up gray space. Place *ruling lines* (horizontal bars above and below the quote) to set it off from the body text. You can also put the pull quote in a box, circle, or any other shape.

Reverse text (white text on a field of gray or black) can be used for pull quotes in the middle of articles, or in corners of pages that need filler material. It is often difficult to read in large quantities, especially if the type size isn't very large. So try to use at least 10-point type, preferably bolded. Avoid typefaces with thin vertical lines (like many serif faces). I find that bold, sans serif type gets the best results since the background's black ink isn't as likely to fill in the letters and clog the type. Very few script or fancy display faces work well for this; these are hard enough to read when they're black on white.

However, *short bursts of* reverse text can be quite dramatic and effective for breaking up long blocks of text and adding visual interest. You need the resources to do it well. This means that the background on your master is a really solid black or gray that doesn't show banding, cross-hatching, or other spottiness. If only an occasional white spot appears on your black background, touch it up with a felt-tip pen. If you're printing from a computer, installing a brand-new toner or ink cartridge can work wonders. I usually keep a spare around for final output just so I can be assured of solid blacks that will reproduce well on the press.

Make sure that the machine that runs your copies is capable of spreading enough ink or fusing enough toner to the page to get solid coverage. Check with your printer, and bring them some sample originals to help them understand what you want.

Type without a computer
You can create headlines via hand-lettering with a pen (if you are talented in this regard), or using sheets of transfer lettering, rub-on letters, or adhesive lettering. Get it from an art store, drafting supply, or paper store. If you buy your lettering from a physical store, rather than online, look around and see if there are any borders (sometimes on tape rolls, sometimes on sheets) or clip-art books that you like. You will probably get more use out of multi-purpose items such as simple borders and insertion art than books on a specific theme. Clip art books or letter sets will cost around $8 per book, though you can find them cheaper. You can often find tasteful ones at garage sales, thrift stores, etc. more frequently than you can find them new at office supply stores. You can find artwork in the darndest places – rummage sales, used book stores, magazines, photos, collages that you make, and just digging through old piles of junk. It's amazing how many gems can be dug up when you are in the mindset of collecting reproducible artwork. Rubber stamps can be great for creating headlines. *Crap Hound* is a great picture-book zine by Sean Tejaratchi that features artwork and typefaces taken from a variety of public domain sources that you can reproduce in your zine.

The cheapest way to produce non-handwritten text is to type it. Manual typewriters can be hard to find, though you can probably pick one up at a garage sale or thrift store if you keep your eyes open. Again, try the online classified sites such as craigslist, or eBay, if you are familiar with what to look for. Despite the ever-present computer, most people don't own a solution for printing on single labels and envelopes, so electric typewriters are still in demand. They're much easier to use than manual models, and most if not all are self-correcting. Try to get a model that will give you some different typeface choices. Test your typewriter before purchasing. Amazingly, you can still find a fair selection of typewriter ribbons in office supply stores.

Headers & Footers

Headers and footers *are fixed text at the top or bottom of each page, like in this book.* They can give a unique feel to your zine. This style works well for zines that are more informational or would appeal to people not accustomed to reading zines. They make a page look more professional, for better or worse. A simple style is to place the name of the zine in the left-page footers, and the issue number into the right-page footers. You can look at different publications to find a style you like.

Paste-up

If you're pasting up pages by hand, I recommend a waxer or a glue stick. I think waxers are better because they allow you the flexibility to move around the elements once you put them down. A waxer is a simple plug-in device that melts wax strips and applies a thin coating to the back of your original when you roll it across. A cheap waxer is adequate for zine work and will set you back maybe $50 new. I found mine at a local paper supply store with decent prices. An inexpensive box of wax strips (maybe $8) seems to last forever. Glue sticks ($1-3) are much cheaper and more portable than a waxer, but it's hard to change placement and they don't last very long.

Glue sticks are better than waxers for putting down small pieces of paper that you're not likely to move. For instance, if you can't get your word processor to number pages properly, just print out the page numbers separately and paste them in. We don't recommend rubber cement or bottled glue – they're messy, and you can ruin your artwork. White glue also dries lumpy.

Besides paper stores, you can try office supply and graphic design stores. You can probably find a local office supply store and make friends with the staff. This is helpful when you have special needs in the future.

Supplies

A transparent ruler ($2 to $3 new) is better than an opaque one. Get the most comfortable, flexible scissors you can find ($3 to $10 if you don't already own ones you like.) I like the Fiskars style with the angled handle. An X-acto knife ($5 to $10) is always handy, sometimes better than scissors. And, if you can afford one, a paper cutter ($15 to $50) is a wonderful tool that simplifies and speeds cutting and trimming (like chopping sheets in half or hacking artwork reductions out of the middle of a sheet of paper).

Also handy: a cutting board, Sharpie markers, non-repro blue pencils (useful for commercial printers), paper trimmer, scanner, and a copier. Bill uses an all-in-one machine that prints, copies, scans, and faxes. Think about borrowing rather than buying larger items that you don't need often.

White out is okay, but only until the brush gets lumpy. It doesn't work well with felt-tip pens; it clogs them up and renders them useless. I highly recommend white correction tape in several different thicknesses or the modern white-out pens, which go on more smoothly than a white-out brush. Even if you use a computer program with a ruling feature, get some black line tape in several point sizes (I like Letraset) for those spots where you just can't get the darn computer to draw the line. A guaranteed headache-saver.

TIP – To avoid pesky lines appearing around the edge of pasted artwork, run a line of white-out along the seam.

a zine can be any size you can think of!

If you shrink or enlarge artwork, get a proportional wheel, which you can buy at an art supply store ($2 to $5). Otherwise, you can probably borrow one from a copy shop, or use a calculator. Enlarging artwork too much can break up the lines; likewise, shrinking can blur them, so test any questionable pieces before it's the last minute and you have no time to play with them. Enlarging digital artwork is almost always a bad idea. See the section on artwork for details on this.

Images

If you can do your own illustration, that's great. Most zinesters use clip art, find someone to illustrate, or both. Look at other zines, for starters, and see whose artwork you like. Perhaps their artist will illustrate for you too, especially if they like what you're doing. I found several illustrators and photographers who saw our zine and contacted us themselves, but when you're starting out, you don't have this advantage. Explain your project to them, with contagious enthusiasm, and they get excited about your stories and articles, and hopefully have some ideas to go with them. Some illustrators are excited to draw pictures from your ideas, while others prefer to come up with the ideas themselves. It's important to make sure you and your illustrator are on the same wavelength about this. If you can pay illustrators, great, but presumably most of us will be asking for donated artwork. Photos are easier to find, simply because most of us can use a camera to create our own images.

Collages can be made of appropriated images from other published material, your own photos, or both, although they usually look best when created from similar material (e.g., all glossy magazines, all cut-up photos, or all newsprint images). Be mindful of copyright violations, but don't obsess. In many cases, your use is reappropriating the intent, meaning, and context of others' work. Many times your use constitutes legal use under the parody clause or fair use. Additionally, your print run is likely not substantial enough to warrant any attention or concern, even if it is technically illegal. You might end up in trouble if the fashion photographer who took the photo doesn't share your keen sense of post-modern irony. On the other hand, if you think you can sneak by, who am I to dampen your creativity? Images become public domain 25 years after their last date of publication.

Rubber stamp prices vary widely. For an extensive supply of cheap stamps, try the crafts section of large toy stores. Custom rubber stamps can be expensive, but they provide a unique look that is hard to duplicate. Decorative hobby stamps are the next most expensive, often in the $6 to $10 range (pads range from $3 to $12). You can make your own using rubber erasers and an X-acto knife. (A detailed guide to doing this and related projects would be the perfect topic for a zine!) There are also mail-order hobbyist suppliers, such as Stamp Francisco.

- Usually it looks better to group similarly created images together on each two-page spread. In other words, be careful about placing clip art, a pencil drawing, and a photograph in the same spread.
- Charts and graphs can illustrate a point effectively.
- A visual representation of information is often more effective at making your point than the most carefully chosen words. Combining text and graphics hammers it home.

Be warned: You will probably discover a typo three minutes before heading out the door to the printer or copy shop. In situations like these, I suggest always correcting the mistake. Why regret not fixing it?

How Do I Do The Cover?

In a store, zines are an impulse item, and most new readers will buy them because they like the cover. So if you're selling in stores, your cover is more important than if you're solely using the mail. Study some other zines and magazines that you like to see how their covers are composed.

If you are having your cover offset printed, it can be a great look to have your image extend off the edge of the page. This is called a bleed. Typicaly a printer requires a bleed to extend 1/4" larger around all 4 edges than the actual size of the cover.

The Title

Popular logic is that the title of your zine should occupy the top two inches of your cover. However, sometimes getting out of the box can aid your zine's appearance and uniqueness. This is an important decision, though, so consult with some folks you trust. Use the largest, widest type possible. This may be the only part of your zine that buyers will notice, and so it should grab their attention. Include the issue number and a price on the cover.

Colors and Images

The most attractive thing you can do with your cover is to use some kind of color – a colored paper stock, color copies, or spot colors on an offset press are all great choices. Aaron Smith has done neat things with photocopiers that have special colors for his zine *Big Hands*. If you find a copy shop with colored toner (not a normal color copier), it is easy, and quite possibly the cheapest and most effective way to do this. Running paper through twice with different colors is even better.

Most zine covers are black and white, so it immediately makes yours visible to include some color. Another important thing to include is an image. Some zinesters, like Shawn Granton of *Ten Foot Rule*, make a sheet of color photocopies to cut up and paste onto the cover of each zine. Sarah of *The Book Bindery* went the opposite route, pasting a black and white photocopy onto the cover of her red-papered zine, which creates a very nice effect as well. Tomas Moniz's zine *Rad Dad* has featured limited-edition letterpress covers by artnoose, giving the zine a really exciting and unique look.

You can have your covers offset printed and still photocopy the guts of your zine. This can be a very economical way to create a great look. With offset, each color increases the price of your printing. Black counts as a color, so in the printing world, a cover with black, red, and yellow would be a three-color job. (You don't count the color of your paper.)

HINT: Use a different color scheme than you used last issue, so that people will immediately know that it's a new issue. Two issues of *The CIA Makes Science Fiction Unexciting* came out about five years apart with the same red and white color scheme. People still think it's the same issue!

If you have a full color image, it can be printed as four separate colors to create full color in print. (Cyan, magenta, yellow, and black, or "CMYK" for short). Sometimes full color printing is cheaper than three colors because it takes less work for someone (or sometimes, you) to separate the colors.

The popularity of color photocopying is also causing prices to drop. If you're doing a photocopied zine, you might consider a full color cover. Sometimes copy shops have specials on color copies. Look for coupons for discounted copy rates.

Other Cover Text
Put some text on the cover explaining the contents of your zine--things that you think are exciting about it. It's good to give people a better idea of what is inside. You can include a list of contributors, features, interviewees, or any particularly interesting, unusual, or topical stories. If you think this will just create clutter, or if the contents wouldn't be recognizable at a glance, it might be better to create a simpler cover with a pleasing design instead. Creating cover text is a great writing exercise to figure out how to say the most with the fewest number of words possible.

Footnotes
1 If you don't have a good local store, you can order most anything on the Internet. Try Arvey Paper / xpedx: https://shop.xpedxstores.com/.
2 *Crap Hound*: $12 from Reading Frenzy, 921 SW Oak St., Portland OR 97205. (503) 274-1449. 11am-7pm, Sun 12pm-6pm. http://www.readingfrenzy.com/
3 Lost Angeles Rubber Works: http://www.larubberworks.com/what.html. For a general directory of online rubber stamp vendors, try: http://www.stampguide.com.
4 Stamp Francisco: http://www.stampfrancisco.com/ "Email is the ONLY way to reach us and ALL orders MUST BE placed via our secure online cart."
[vLetter, www.signaturesoftware.com. **Phone:** 541-387-2800 (8am to 4pm Pacific Time, Monday through Friday, closed on holidays). **Email:** service@vLetter.com. **Fax:** 503-296-2429]

photos, illustration, & pre-press

You can really improve the immediacy of your zine if you take a decent picture to dramatize a story or article. Of course, one alternative is to get a photographer friend to take pictures for you, but it's easier to be able to do it yourself whenever you want.

This section is not a photography primer. It only covers the basics of good b/w photography. Any good camera shop should stock a selection of manuals that cover the topic in detail. Bill likes the book <u>A Short Course in Photography</u> by Barbara London. Joe likes the zine *Scrim Shank*. Both are introductions to good b/w photographic and composition techniques. Investigate your local library for the book that is perfect for you.

Most people no longer use film cameras and a good digital camera can be purchased for about $100-400. Be sure to read any instructions that come with your camera, to learn about any special capabilities it may have.

Considerations when Photographing

To make sure your photos don't come out too light or dark, I suggest bracketing them. This means you take up to three shots of your subject at what you believe the ideal exposure to be; one at the setting just above that; and one at the setting just below that. Digital cameras have a preview screen that will help you judge if you have a usable shot.

Most people shoot too far from the subject; thus, their photos have too much going on in the background. Get as tight a focus as possible, so you have the most information to work with after your photo is developed.

The more controlled your lighting is, the better. Learn to use a flash indoors. Remember that your eyes adjust to dimness, but cameras don't. Use lots of light to avoid a muddy, grayed-out image. Avoid shooting into the sun. Ideally, the sun is behind you or off to one side.

If you want to use someone else's photos or artwork, review the copyright section to make sure you aren't getting yourself into trouble. More than anything else, respect your peers! It's one thing to steal photos from a high-end magazine or use expired public domain, but it is another altogether to use the work of your peers without even asking.

Adobe Photoshop, or its open-source freeware variant Gimp, is the ideal computer program for photo and graphic manipulation. You can import your photos direct from your camera and resize them. You can also correct contrast and brightness problems as well as convert photos to black and white. As a starting point, I usually turn both the brightness and contrast up 20 points. It may look washed-out on your screen, but usually won't on paper. If you are dealing with film photos, you can put them in your scanner to import them into Photoshop or Gimp. There are many books devoted to these programs, as well as a large community of users who maintain online discussion forums. The manual isn't bad, either.

You can use color photos in a black and white zine, but you'll want to convert them first. Taking photos in black and white captures a greater degree of contrast than color. Color photos often become gray and washed-out when translated into b/w. The biggest problem I notice when using color photos is that by the time the image gets sent through the press, the darker grays usually print black. Most offset presses that print zines are good at contrast and not so good at subtlety and nuance. Photocopiers sometimes have an advantage in this regard, especially with you at the helm.

Most photocopiers now just have a photo setting, where you can place a color or black and white photo on the copier, turn on the photo setting, and it'll give you a reproducible copy. You can lighten or darken this print as needed, and what you see is what you get, unlike on a computer screen.

If you are importing or scanning photos for your zine, you'll want to have your final images at least 300 dots-per-inch (DPI) and at the final print size. DPI is exactly what it says, the number of dots per inch that are used to create a composite image to the eye. You can't enlarge digital photos without a rapid loss in quality.

A **halftone** *is an image setting, most commonly used for photos, where a field of intermittent tiny black dots are used to resemble gray*, like you see in newspaper photos. A copier or press cannot accurately photocopy grays and normally muddies them or makes them too dark and indecipherable. The halftone process allows photos to be reproduced consistently and legibly. Some folks like Keith Rosson and Aaron Cometbus also use blown up halftone patterns as an aesthetic design.

Your printer will typically be the best one to setup your halftones for you. If they would like you to do it, it's still fairly easy. In Gimp or Photoshop, pull down the "image" menu, select "mode", and choose "bitmap". If bitmap is not an option, first chose "grayscale" and then go back and choose "bitmap". One of your options is "halftone screen". Choose that and it'll prompt your output resolution and dot pattern. Ask your printer for these. Most printers prefer a "round" dot pattern and can direct you regarding the proper line screen.

HINTS: Paper and ink make a difference. If your material comes back consistently too dark, ask the printer to turn down the ink flow on the press. You can also go back and adjust brightness and contrast in Photoshop. If you're using a layout program like Scribus, Quark, or InDesign, set your halftone images to 85% shade rather than the default 100%. You can also try screening your images at a lower line density. This can get confusing so it's best to have printers set it up themselves or tell you the proper setting for optimum output. Photos with high contrast tend to work best.

You'll need to create a "camera ready" master to run through the copier. Whether you do this by printing a copy from your computer or by creating the master on paper is up to you. Some photocopy shops can even handle printing out a PDF through their digital photocopying equipment.

As of 2003, 99% of commercial printers prefer (and charge less for) a single PDF file of your finished zine. If your zine is primarily hand made and your finished work is on sheets of paper (rather than a file), you will want to submit it to the printer "camera-ready". "Camera-ready" used to mean providing finished pages that a printer would shoot with a giant stat camera. Today, your zine would most likely be scanned into a computer or run through a photocopier.

If you print in color, inquire about the best way to turn in your images. Most places will want each color as a separate page, file, or Photoshop channel. Inquire with your printer about how they want the files before you start preparing your cover. If you are printing full color CMYK, it is much easier, as you just convert your pages in Photoshop or Gimp by going to "Image", "Mode", "CMYK" and it's ready for print! You can also learn to colorize black and white images either manually or with the help of computer software, after scanning an image into a computer. You can create some very nice surrealistic effects this way.

printing and paper

Most zines are stapled twice through all of the pages along the middle fold. A saddle stapler seems to have a little more strength than a long-arm one. It staples on the spine after you've already folded your zine. A long arm staples before you've folded it in half. Either one is really only built to staple through about 10-15 sheets of paper (40-60 pages).

Most printers have in-house binding capabilities, while some shop out this part of the job. If you're photocopying a short run, you can assemble the zines yourself. All you really need is a long-arm stapler and the time and patience to assemble them. Or you could pay for folding and still do the stapling yourself. This is usually the most expensive part of assembly cost, as it can cost several cents per staple. Make sure your job isn't too thick for your stapler.

HINT: You can see if a copy shop has an electric saddle stapler. Maybe you can use it; but it helps to make some copies first, and then hit them up for the stapler. The electric saddle staplers have a foot switch that pulls staples from a spool of wire – simple and easy. With a bit of practice, you can get fairly good at this. If they don't have an electric saddle stapler, they may have a manual stapler you can use.

In Portland, Walker Copy did pickups, deliveries, and had the best price in town. Not surprisingly, their machines eventually died and they couldn't afford to fix or replace them. In Bloomington we use a local copy shop that charges us 3 cents per side. You can probably find something comparable where you live. It makes

the most sense to do photocopying locally, unless you have a totally free hookup somewhere else.

Aside from stapling, there are a few other options you might consider. There are comb and wire spiral binding systems available at copy shops. If it fits your aesthetic, a sharp-looking comb binding can help your zine stand out and sit flat when it's being read. An Ibico comb binding system is a good simple solution to use at a home. This is particularly useful for cook zines and how-to manuals.

Any kind of paper-fastening system could work for a zine. How about using a three-prong folder as a cover? They come in colors, and you could paste a color-photocopy inset onto the cover. Round metal brads, safety pins, and sewing are other possibilities. I've seen zines bound with string or rubber bands, but the latter is a bad idea as they become brittle and break.

Christoph Meyer of *28 Pages Lovingly Bound with Twine* is the king of binders, because, as you might imagine, he really does hand-tie each copy three times with pieces of twine. The exception to this was the dental issue, which was bound with dental floss. Being creative like this is what is so empowering about zines. You have a wealth of options.

Collating
Collating is the process of putting the pages in order. You can have your zine collated or do it yourself. Many photocopiers can automatically print on both sides of the page (called "double sided") and collate themselves if they are setup properly before you start copying. You should double check about this first, as this will save many hours of work.

Folding
You can have the sheets folded or do that yourself. I only recommend the extra work if you have a very short print run — say, under 200 zines — and relatively few pages. It saves a little money, but it's a heck of a lot of work and it can be quite frustrating. Folding is a chore for anything over 24 pages. You can alleviate that somewhat by using a bone-folder (the proper tool), stick or other flat object to make

the fold for you. Believe it or not, that's how printers still do it too, unless they have a booklet maker, which does all of the folding, binding, and trimming automatically.

Trimming

If your zine is very thick, then you can give it a hot look by having it trimmed along the vertical edge. When you fold a lot of sheets, the outside sheets are going to be stick out less than the inside sheets. Thus, you end up with progressively "shorter" edges the further out you go. It's like running on the outside track in a track field or driving along the outside lane of a freeway curve. Notice how they stagger runners or cars in a race? It's the same principle. Most printers or copy shops will trim your zine for a small charge.

Folding and stapling 500 zines could reasonably take about 16-20 hours of your time. You may find that part of the job joyous or laborious. Act accordingly!

Printing

How you print your zine depends two variables. (1) How many copies do you want? 100-200 copies is a good starting place unless you need more for a special reason. (2) How much money do you have to spend on printing? The more colors and pages, the more it will cost.

If you're printing 500 copies or less, it probably makes the most sense to use a photocopier. This has several advantages: you can print as many or as few copies as you want; it's easy to make more if you run out of the first batch; it saves you money and commitment to an expensive offset run; and you can get the finished copies back pretty quickly. On the other hand, if you end up making 1,000 copies of your zine, photocopying can be expensive and time-consuming, especially when you include collating, folding, and stapling. Even 500 can be a lot, depending on how long your zine is.

If you have access to free copying, then you'll be printing your zine on that photocopier until your print runs are too large. Be creative with your copying. Use colored paper for the cover, and maybe even inside, if it looks good. If you're doing a small print run, there are a couple of ways to add color to your cover without spending too much money: (1) Use a quarter of a single sheet as an inset on each cover for a digest-size zine, pasting it onto the front of each copy with a glue stick. (2) Use colored pencils, highlighters, or magic markers to hand-color the line art on your cover. (3) Run a screen print on top of your photocopied cover or make a simple stencil.

Offset printing is a lithographic process, meaning that ink and water are run through cylinders and cling to the parts of the paper where the press indicates. This is done by creating films from your artwork that are used to make printing plates that tell the printing press exactly what your zine will look like. It is easy and cheap once the films and plates are made, but the handling of them and setting up the press is the troublesome and expensive part. If a page uses more than one color, it uses a corresponding amount of films and plates.

Three good offset printers are 1984 Printing in Oakland, CA, Parcell Press in Richmond, VA, and Eberhardt Press in Portland, OR. All three are familiar with zines and the kinds of questions you would have.

www.1984printing.com
www.parcellpress.com
www.eberhardtpress.org

These are typically the best places to start, as all are reasonably priced and suited to small runs (500-3,000). It is improbable that you would ever be doing larger runs than that, and if you do, you may become more knowledgeable than we are! The two printers that Microcosm uses for larger runs are United Graphics in Mattoon, IL and Lebonfon in Quebec, who specialize in graphic novels and won't be scared away by complicated artwork. They do print runs of 3,000-10,000.

Call as many printers as possible. I've called up to two dozen printers for quotes on a job. Compare quotes and share quotes between printers. Judging capabilities of various printers helps you save money, and increases your knowledge. Each printer has different strengths and weaknesses. There are three main factors of printing – (1) print quality, (2) turnaround time, (3) cost. Common wisdom dictates that no printer can provide all three, but this is false. It can be done! You must also consider how pleasant it is to deal with your printer. This can be a total deal breaker.

Whenever you have a question, don't be afraid to ask. It's your money, and you're paying the printer to guide you. All my printers have given me valuable tips, helping to save time and money. For instance, some printers know a lot about photo and halftoning processes and can help make your photos look even better. Each printer has a unique set of requirements and preferences. Get to know their formats and their flexibilities.

Try to become friendly with your printer from the get-go. This will be more valuable than you can dream of. They'll be more likely to cut you slack on the price and payments. Don't piss them off by breaking agreements (like delivery dates) and bringing them unfinished work that requires extra coddling on their part. At all times, communicate clearly about your printing needs. Get samples of the paper stock and some of their finished print work. Get prices for color and halftones.

On rare occasion, a printer will refuse to print your material because they found the content objectionable. You can prevent this by asking if they would have a problem printing something outrageous, such as obscene words or something incendiary or politically radical. Think of the most obscene graphic image you would ever consider publishing, and ask if it would be a problem. It's better to find out up front than after you drop off your job.

HINT: For offset printing, it always helps to compare different zines and see how they were done. If you like the print job on a particular zine, find out who their printer is. If they're no longer using that printer, find out why.

HINT: Find out whether you can get "overs" at no extra charge. "Overs" are extra copies shops print to cover their mistakes. One thing you can try is to order extra covers; if they've got the extra copies, they just might bind them into those covers at no extra cost.

How do I get a offset price quote?
Email your printers with all of your specifications: number of pages, finished size (width x height), type of paper, type of cover and binding you want, and the number of copies you want, number of colors on the cover, special effects (such as varnishes or gatefold covers), how you will deliver the final master, and where you want them shipped to. Request a turnaround time estimate also. With most printers this is consistent for every job, but they will sometimes complete it early.

If your zines will be printed on a printing press there is an important distinction to make from using a copy machine. A signature is the number of pages from your zine that fit onto one parent printing sheet. For example, 32 pages often fit a press at 5x7" and means that a multiple of 32 makes for an efficient price and printing job. If you had slightly more or less pages it could affect the price drastically. Talk to your printer about this and find a good size and coordinating page count.

While most printers use a signature of 16 pages or 32 pages, zine sized printers sometimes have a 4 page signature. Always ask what would yield a better price for the same amount of content. Changing your page size or page count may drastically improve your price.

Always get multiple quotes from each printer with different page counts or different print quantities. This will allow you to see how their pricing structure works, in a simple way that is applicable to your zine printing. Prices usually vary widely between printers, even within the same town, so always get at least 2 or 3 quotes. The main reason for this is that the same print job will fit differently on each press. Also different printers will specialize in different lengths and quantities to attract different types of customers.

There are many variables in a print job, so keep an open mind. Sometimes it may cost less to print 2,000 copies than 1,500. If you can get your zine printed on a web press (that uses giant rolls of paper instead of single sheets), you may see a dramatic drop in the price per copy.

HINT: Sometimes you can save on postage if you can use a paper that will cause your zine to weigh less. Some printers charge much less for a lighter paper than for heavier stock, but don't count on it. If you have heavy ink coverage, you may need a heavier paper to keep black areas from showing through. Paper pricing depends on the printer – how they're pricing their jobs, and what kinds of breaks they're getting on paper – which, aside from labor, is normally their largest expense.

Variety costs money. If you use more than one color of ink or type of paper, inserts that do not conform to the zine's size, an unusual size requiring trimming, etc., you will pay extra.

Can I offset in full color?
It is much more expensive per copy, but sometimes you'll have a project that requires it, like artwork reproductions or photographs. There's no such thing as truly cheap full color printing, but online print-on-demand companies like lulu.com offer a service where you can order 100, 10, or 1 copy per printing. It may cost you $4-$20 per copy, but this is sometimes a viable option, if you don't have a lot of money to invest in it. An offset full color print job for an entire zine is prohibitively expensive. Most major publishers print full color jobs or hardcover books in the third world – Hong Kong, Singapore, or China. These countries offer pricing that makes it more feasible to print in color, taking advantage of often cheap, forced labor. Obviously, most people would take immediate ethical issue with this. We have discovered that there are several cost effective full color printers in Italy and were pleasantly surprised by some of the quotes that we got from United Graphics as well.

The reason that full color offset is so expensive is because each page requires four passes through the printer, once for each of the subtractive primary colors: cyan, magenta, yellow, and black. All the other colors are combinations of the above four. This is called *process color* and is a very exacting process to align or register each color perfectly over the previous one.

There is also *Pantone color*. Pantone Matching System (PMS) is a color matching system that assigns a number to every shade of a color, enabling you to specify very precise colors to your printer, in a universal language. This is used if you are just printing 2 or 3 colors instead of full color. Think of a pantone like a paint sample.

HINT: Pantones often look very different on screen than they do on paper. Get samples.

Once you start using color on the cover, it doesn't seem like such a big cost, since you just factor it in from the outset. If you want to do a short run (under 1,000 copies) of a zine with a full color cover only, you might find a printer who does digital short-run printing without plates or films, like on a high-end color copier. It will not match offset quality, but it's a good and fairly inexpensive option if you print on high-quality paper.

HINT: Here's a trick you can use to achieve extra colors and a pretty cool look without paying for it. If you are printing red, you can get pink for free by making those areas of red only 10% color. This can work especially well with background colors, where this pastel effect is common.

Don't print full color just for the sake of full color. It can often look tacky. It takes time, practice, and effort to learn to do it properly. I would recommend starting with a simple spot PMS color. I would suggest mastering the use of two colors before experimenting with four. Many publications look best just sticking with 2 or 3 color covers.

Some zinesters who do full color have their covers printed by a different printer than the one who does the inside sheets. Different printers have different presses, different staffs, and correspondingly different strengths and weaknesses. By asking about their specific setup, you'll become better educated about printing processes and options, and make better decisions about how to print your zines. Even different photocopiers have varying capabilities.

If your printer can't do the cover you want (which can be the case, for instance, if they're strictly a newsprint shop and you want a glossy cover), they may still be able to shop it out at a better price than you can get alone.

HINT: If you do use more than one ink color, keep in mind that there are ways to save on that, too. Make sure that you maximize the possibilities of spot color and screens. Let's say you have a two-color cover. The colors are black and red on white paper. That means that you can also use red on your back cover, since that's the same sheet as the front cover.

What kind of paper should I use? For photocopying, everyday 20-pound bond stock should suffice. The "pound" designation is based on the weight in pounds of a case of letter-sized sheets. You may want to consider a card stock for the cover if the machine can handle it (67-lb. works well; 80-lb. is even sturdier). If you're going with offset printing, I recommend a smooth rather than a vellum finish, as it will make your pictures look better. Start with a 50 or 60-lb. text stock. If your zine has a lot of heavily saturated black areas start with 60-lb.

Some zinesters like Andalusia of the radical women's bicycle zine *Clitical Mass,* print their zines entirely on the back of already printed paper that is truly 100% post consumer, instead of recycling it. This requires a lot of found paper but is a great way to lower the global impact of your publishing.

New Leaf is a paper distribution company that uses 100% post-consumer recycled paper (rather than just recycling paper off the print shop floor). Ask your printer what 100% PCW papers they have in stock. There are other kinds of completely tree-free paper like Kenaf that you may want to investigate as well.

Some zinesters hate newsprint with a passion, while others swear by it. If you're giving away your zine, and the point is to give away as many copies as possible, then newsprint will probably be the cheapest way to go. Supposedly less ink rubs off of higher-grade white newsprint; so consider using that instead of the cheapest stuff.

While newsprint is much cheaper for larger runs than regular paper, it's low quality and falls apart. The print quality is also inferior on newsprint, since the ink can't get as deep into the paper. Blacks will always look gray. This is something you may be able to live with. If you're producing an arty zine with a lot of emphasis on visuals, you may be better off with a nice photocopy job than a smudgy newsprint one. Newsprint doesn't last for long and has a more disposable feel to it, so people are more likely to toss your zine without reading it. Ask yourself how much you like reading newsprint publications, and go from there.

Slug & Lettuce and *Maximum RocknRoll* are two long-running punk zines (23 and 26 years running, respectively) that both always print on newsprint. This is a mixed bag. For archival purposes, these zines will be much harder to preserve, but in the sense of their scale and distribution, this makes sense. Slug & Lettuce gives away the entire print run of 10,000 copies and pays for printing by selling advertisements. *Maximum RocknRoll* has a $4 cover price and prints thousands of copies of each issue. They have adamantly stuck to their original aesthetic and refuse to use a stock cover. This works for them and their appearance is very unique. *MRR* sets the aesthetic standard for a DIY punk fanzine. However, it does not mail very well without a protective cover and copies frequently arrive ripped.

HINT: Often times your local newspaper will be a cheap place to print your zine in their downtime between printing the daily news.

Other zines like *Power of a Question* employ such complicated folding and specialized assembly that the only option is photocopying on normal paper and cover stock.

Cometbus is a good example of a zine that uses large scale offset printing without adopting the visual trappings of a magazine. Around 12,000 copies of each issue are printed on white paper, more or less resembling a nicely trimmed photocopied black-and-white zine.

Because photocopied zines have much simpler choices in many senses than offset or newsprint zines, we've contacted some people who have worked with offset on their zines for some time to help you make better-informed choices.

Jackson Ellis of Verbicide, Christine Boarts of Slug & Lettuce, and Todd Taylor of Razorcake talk about printing!

1) What is your print run, how much does it cost, and how many of those copies are given away for free versus sold on a newsstand or otherwise?

Verbicide: Other than a couple boxes of house copies per issue that we keep for web store sales, *Verbicide* is entirely free. We circulate it in as many cities and venues as we can afford. I used to say that we'd send it to anyone who'd take as many copies as they could move, but I can't keep up with the demand. 25,000 copies is my benchmark; generally, as any publisher will tell you, the revenue stream dictates press run more than any other factor. I could *easily* move 40,000 or 50,000 copies. Our pick-up rate is nearly 100%.

Slug & Lettuce: It costs about $1,800 to print 10,000 copies for a 20 page tabloid size. The zine is free—in person, or available for postage costs—whether a single copy or a bundle or box of copies. Some issues I have only a handful of copies left, and some I have hundreds left over. Some seasons I get to more shows and events and more bands pass through, while other seasons are quieter. For the most part—I get rid of most of the copies of each issue and hold on to enough for the archives.

Razorcake: Here are some quick estimates:

Printing: $2,800, Supplies for shipping (boxes, tape, labels): $300, Postage: $2,000

These numbers change with every issue. We have a comprehensive protocol so we don't over-buy or under-buy supplies, nor do we over-run or under-run the zine. Postage has been in a lot of flux the past two years. (Media mail is restricted, Bound Printed Matter is by pre-postage only, surface international was eliminated, etc.)

We have stopped negotiating with all national chain accounts. We deal with a select few traditional distributors. We have a subscriber base of 1,000. We send approximately 3,500 for distribution (all the way from local mom and pops to international stores. It's very important to have a constantly updated database for this.) We donate to two book-for-prisoner programs. We donate to other non-profit centers, teen centers, and libraries. We also keep some aside for benefits, either for Razorcake or for other causes. At the end of an issue's rotation, we usually have 100 copies on hand to satisfy new subscribers and new orders.

2) Why have you adopted this strategy?

Razorcake: Because traditional, national magazine distribution is dying. Unless you're selling over 50,000 copies, chances are you'll never be paid. We were associated with two large independent distributors: Desert Moon, then Big Top. Both went out of business owing people a lot of money, and taking many independent publications down with them. We were on top of both situations, and walked away from both largely unscathed because we saw the warning signs and pulled out as soon as our contract allowed. Don't be afraid to press people who legitimately owe you money.

Slug & Lettuce: It came about partly out of necessity — 18 years ago or so, I was printing how ever many copies of a one page zine as I could afford to and then just giving them away at shows. It built from there. Selling zines was hard to do. Getting enough money to print a big zine was hard. I simplified that process by making it smaller and what I could afford. It grew exponentially from there—more copies, more pages as I could afford it. The zine being free has been essential ever since, enabling it to be spread wide and far and therefore further promoting the networking and communication aspect without relying on purchasing it.

Verbicide: Several reasons. First, I can't stand working with distributors. I worked with distributors for seven years. What a waste of time. They never deliver on promises; routinely do the bare minimum to help move copies. The ones who don't withhold thousands of dollars from you are the ones who overcharge you in every conceivable fashion. The smaller/regional distros seemed to maintain a level of communication, honesty, and respect—and payment schedule— and that's not enough to sustain a business. Chain retailers are also killing small publishing companies. This isn't some reflexive anti-corporate statement, and I'm not being reactionary or holding a grudge—I mean that after years of dealing with chains and their distributors, it's apparent that if you can't afford to pay up, you're not going to get a fair shot to succeed in the country's biggest outlets. If you can't pay up, you're expected to maintain an unrealistic sell-through percentage. I'm so glad that I've simplified my business, simplified my *life*, and stopped wasting so many copies. Dan Sinker from *Punk Planet* once quipped, that he would have saved a lot of money and trouble if he'd just received thousands of copies per issue and immediately loaded them into a dumpster.

Secondly—relating to the unsold copies—*Verbicide* is a magazine that I want to be enjoyed and read by as many people as possible. Why the hell would I want 70% of the copies going into retail to end up in the trash? I'd rather give them away.

As I said, the demand is there. We used to print between 8,000 and 16,000 copies for years when we were retail—and *thousands* of those were trashed. Now we do upwards of 25k each issue and nearly every copy ends up read. That is awesome to me. I wish I could double my circulation and page count, but as it is, I'm limited by funding. Most labels are either tanking or simply don't know what the fuck they're doing, and they misappropriate funding these days to outsourced PR companies who carpet-bomb the industry with hundreds of unread spam messages a day, or they pay four times the price we charge to a glossy magazine with a much bigger press run who, at the end of the day, due to average sell-through rates, probably don't move many more actual copies than *Verbicide*. It's frustrating as hell.

3) What percentage of your print costs are covered by advertising?

Verbicide: Less than 100%, and it's *Verbicide*'s only source of income, with the exception of a small bit of cash from online sales, and our CD sampler, which I started solely to pick up some of the slack in the lagging print ad sales so I could keep *Verbicide* in print.

Razorcake: 100%. Our advertising rate covers printing and shipping. That was by design. We need that money to pick up and ship off the zine. Neither our printer nor the USPS work on credit.

Slug & Lettuce: The advertising money pays for the printing costs and a percentage of postage money for shipping out the trade copies (everyone who has a review receives a copy) as well as a certain amount of copies that were sent to distributors. S&L paid for itself, but never actually made any money.

4) What are some other ways that you raise money?

Slug & Lettuce: I've made t-shirts, patches, coffee mugs and posters. Believe it or not I've never once had a benefit show. I've also had many generous donations over the years— whether it's a book of stamps or $100—every little bit helped.

Razorcake: We are a book publisher, a record company, and a distributor of others' works (mostly vinyl records). It's mainly set up through our website, www.razorcake.org. The combination of all of our projects allow us to stay afloat. We also are fortunate enough to have periodic benefits thrown in our name.

5) How much have these factors changed in the last few years?

Slug & Lettuce: Things have changed enormously! First of all, no one has any money anymore, period. Whereas once upon a time it was not that difficult to get the ads in S&L, year by recent year that has become harder and harder. And then year by year the postage rates have gone up and up. Last year the postage rate increased by 400% for international packages, which essentially now makes it impossible for me to send bundles of S&L overseas. Whereas before I could send 10 pounds (aprox 70 copies) for about $10, it is now at least $40! And that is just not economical or affordable to anyone. So the double whammy has really been hard.

Verbicide: When *Verbicide* was earning twice as much money in ad sales, I was putting it all back into the magazine. *Verbicide* was frequently between 80 and 88 pages, which costs a lot more than 48 pages, which we are currently at and can barely afford. Rising shipping costs have really hurt us, too. Shipping prices have almost doubled since 2002. Basically, we just work with what we have. Scissor Press has never had an office or paid employees; my partner Nate and I have never drawn a salary. I just turned 28—I started *Verbicide* when I was 19. I'm not naïve, and I realize that certain things in life *are* about money. I would love to have some money, and I would love to earn it with *Verbicide*. But it's not about money; I can hope and wish and work as hard as possible, but until it becomes impossible to break even, I'll keep doing it. I'll do it if we have to print only 24 pages and 5,000 copies. Whatever. If advertisers want to bail on us, fine. Our readers will at least know that 24 pages or 80 pages, we're putting the best content we can into the space we can afford.

6) Why did you decide on the kinds of cover and paper stock that you use?

Verbicide: Because it's affordable. I used to get hung up on using heavy paper (issue 7 was a coffee table-style sheet-fed book that cost about $1.10 per copy to print!), and I used to be obsessed with the notion of going glossy someday. It seemed like that was the thing to do, the way to succeed, and I was jealous of zines like *Law of Inertia* when they jumped to glossy; I had an inferiority complex when I saw *Verbicide* on the shelf next to *Rockpile, Chord, Devil In The Woods, Clamor, Amplifier, Lollipop, Harp, No Depression, Fat City, Caustic Truths, Resonance, Snaggletooth*, and other magazines that were glossy and now are out of business.

Now I'm more pragmatic in my approach. We work with a sick printer; I can't believe how nice of a job they do. Our material is relatively inexpensive, but we get the most for our dollar. By keeping the overhead down we can keep ad rates down, and, in theory, we won't be in over our heads if we had a massive glossy magazine budget.

Slug & Lettuce: In the early 90s, as the one sheet format of S&L was growing, I knew some people who were printing on tabloid newsprint—the prices were reasonable and so I made a jump to that. At the time I printed 1,000 copies of a one piece of newsprint 4 sheet tabloid paper for about $150 (at the time that was a chunk of money out of my pocket—now it sounds like nothing). Then it increased in pages and copies in increments till I reached 10,000 copies and 20 pages. I essentially capped myself at that due to weight and postage. 20 pages weighed in just under 2 oz, which I could then send for a 2 oz first class stamp. (50-60cents in the past 10 years or so). If the weight went up to 3 oz, then all of a sudden it was more like 75cents and rather than 7 copies in a pound it was 5, and so the whole fragile financial structure of keeping the zine FREE started to crumble. Hence I made the type smaller and smaller to continue to fit more and more into the pages, while keeping it free, something which was essential. I would have loved to have used a nicer grade of paper which for one thing would have held the tones for the photographs much better, and also would have been cleaner on the hands reading it, but alas higher grade of paper costs more and weighs more and so it was not an option.

Razorcake: If you make over 1,000 copies of a zine, it's much cheaper, per unit, to go offset newsprint. We went with that. The first issue had a newsprint cover. Too many of them were damaged in the mail, so we went with a glossy cover with issue #2. We went to bright newsprint three years back because I like seeing clearer photos in print. We use solely local businesses for all of our printing. (Covers and insides are done at different locations.)

7) How have you learned from similar publications and their decisions?

Slug & Lettuce: At some point year and years ago I saw a "presort bulk postage" box on a zine I got in the mail, I asked the zine maker about that—he told me all about the bulk mail permit and how if you presort the mail you get a discount, so long as you are sending at least 250 pieces at once. I looked into that and did that, which saved some money on postage. The newsprint format that I used was originally introduced to me by the *Squat or Rot* publication, I researched it, it worked out for me. When I moved out of NYC I wasn't sure what I'd do. *The Defenstrator* in Philly hooked me up with a printer (Prompt Press) in Camden NJ that had great prices and shipped via Amtrak to Richmond. When *Profane Existence* was printing some spot color on their newsprint covers—I thought that was pretty cool—looked into it, found out it cost more than was affordable for me and passed. Over the years I have compared mailing lists, printers, formats, mailing and shipping rates, all that sort of stuff with other zine folks who were doing similiar things. Essentially I have always felt that I had a thousand resources on hand through the network of friends and other zine makers around the world. I see something that looks like it works, ask about it, look into and see what happens. Or I see something that doesn't and remember it.

Razorcake: I know what works for us—like putting nothing on credit, doing only projects we have the money for in hand, and slowly gaining speed is the best method for us. After seven years, I'm still working on new aspects to how to run the zine more effectively and efficiently without losing any perspective on why we started it in the first place.

FlightCheck, recommended for error-checking of digital files before sending to printer: http://www.thepowerxchange.com/product_7615_detailed.html
"FlightCheck Designer (formerly FlightCheck Collect) is a stand-alone application that assists designers as well as service providers in preflighting all major desktop-publishing files. $199 in Mac and Win formats; $99 for upgrades. Available from: ThePowerXChange, PO Box 2049, Wheat Ridge CO 80034. Phone: (877) 940-0600 (toll-free) or (303) 940-0600 (local/int'l). Fax: (303) 940-0601. Email: sales@thepowerxchange.com

BLOCK PRINTING
instructions

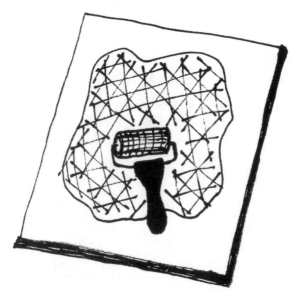

Blockprinting is a very simple way to add texture and color to your zine pages - particularly your covers! It takes a little more time and love than photocopying, but it's something special. Here are Eleanor Whitney's simple instructions for adding blockprinting to your zine!

Learning to Block Print.............

1. Obtain a slab of linoleum, rubber, or like material. Obtain "cutting tools." These items are readily available at art stores.

2. Using a pencil, draw your design onto a slab of material. Then, use cutting tools (safety first!) to cut out either the marks you made w/ your pencil <u>or</u> the surrounding areas. The areas you <u>don't</u> cut are the ones that will print. Therefore, if you want a positive of your image, cut out the surrounding area of your pencil marks. If you want a negative of your image, cut out your pencil marks. Different types of cutting tools achieve various sorts of cuts. Test out your tools & skills on extra slabs of material before you cut into your drawing.

3. Inking your block up cleanly & smoothly might take a bit of practice. Recommended ink for use is water soluable kinds because these lend well for clean-up & don't emit harmful fumes. Obtain a small (8x8 inches, for example) piece of plexiglass & squirt about two teaspoons of your ink of choice on it. Obtain a small rubber roller (also available at art stores) and evenly distribute ink onto plexi with it. "Evenly distribute" = ink should be spread thin all over plexi & the rubber roller's interaction w/ ink & plexi will create an unmistakeable "ch-ch-ch" sound.

4. Now, take your roller fully loaded w/ it's smooth layer of ink & apply it evenly to the surface of your lineoleum, rubber, or block

material.

5. Place the paper / cardstock / whatever you are printing onto over the inked block & don't move it! (Smears ruin designs.) Press hard onto paper with a wooden spoon or brayer (art store item) until you think that our design has successfully transferred onto your surface.

5. Carefully lift up a corner to check if your design really has transferred. If it has not, put corner back down without moving anything, & continue pressing & rubbing. If it has successfully transferred lift your surface (paper, etc.) off the block surface in one full, careful swoop!

6. Put your print in a safe place to dry. Repeat steps 4 & 5 until you have your desired # of prints. You will have to keep adding ink in small amounts to plexi w/ roller in order to keep you ink on roller fresh & flowing.

7. Clean-up! If you used water-soluable ink you can wash your block carving with warm, soapy water & blot dry. If you used oil-based ink, use turpentine / mineral spirits & paper towel to rub surface clean. (And dispose of your flammable paper towels!)

8. Congratulations! You are a block printer!

SO, TELL ME YOUR BIGGEST FEAR...

interviews

Interviews are a wonderful way to add variety to your zine, convey a point in a stronger way, or bring in readers excited about a certain person, band, subculture, or organization. This section is intended to help you along the way.

Doing an interview can be very time-consuming and labor-intensive, so be sure to have lots of lead time before you plunge in. If you want to print very soon and there's another way to fill the space, it might be better to wait until next issue to print the interview. You will also get a better result when both you and the subject are relaxed. Rushing will probably leave you stressed and frustrated, unless the interview and the space to be filled are very brief.

There are typically two reasons to do an interview. One is to profile an interesting personality, band, or organization; the other is to get quotes from a credible source to substantiate points your zine is trying to make.

In the mid-90s hey-day of zines, it was very common to find throwaway quality interviews with popular indie bands in zines. The questions frequently lacked depth or thought, and the discussion would always seem to wind down as soon as it went anywhere. Partially because of this, interviews gained a reputation as filler content, and were largely ignored by readers.

More recently there's been a healthy resurgance of interview based zines. In *Identity Crisis,* Lauren interviews a dozen of her peers who have extensive knowledge and experience in the punk scene—creating a composite of different lifestyles within our subculture. The long-running *Duplex Planet* interviews elderly people living in retirement homes and prints their acquired wisdom. Aaron Cometbus interviewed employees at a worker-owned coffee shop in issue #46. In the "Back to the Land" issue he interviews numerous adults who were raised collectively and rurally. He documents this movement and creates a composite view of experiences that require no additional narrative.

The beauty of the interview format is that it allows you to have someone else making or substantiating your points. It also makes for interesting reading when you have several people with multiple points of view.

There are typically four ways to do an interview – in person, over the phone, by writing letters, or via e-mail.

E-mail is the least labor intensive as you can paste the finished results right into your zine. Letter writing is typically reserved for subjects that have no other way of being interviewed (they live far away with no phone or e-mail). Some people do prefer this method though. In-person interviews are best for understanding the nuances of your subject and playing off their non-verbal responses. It also offers the best opportunities for follow-up, conversation-style questions. Telephone interviews are easier to schedule than in-person interviews and can offer similar results. They are also good for follow-up interviews.

Do your homework. Familiarize yourself with the subject's work and read other interviews they've given. Run a basic google search online and see what background facts you can find. Sometimes you will be more nervous than the subject. Going in prepared and informed will help reduce that.

Prepare 6-10 questions ahead of time, and leave room for some degree of spontaneity. You don't want to sound like you're reading from a script and not acknowledging their responses. I normally add another 6-10 questions (time permitting) during the course of the interview to help it feel more conversational.

Be on time. If you must be late, then call. Try to estimate how much time it'll take in advance and stick to it. You want to respect other people's time.

If you are recording by phone or in person, running a quick level check on the recorder is important. Don't leave out this step. It only takes a minute or two. You don't want to take someone's time taping an interview, only to find out that everything is inaudible and useless. Learn how to use your recorder before you attempt to rely on it for an interview.

Let the subject do most of the talking, unless they need directed a little bit or you have something really compelling to say. Reacting is fine, but try not to laugh or make too many noises over their speech; this can distract them and makes it hard to understand later. Turn away for a moment if you have to cough, sneeze, or make other loud noises that the recorder may pick up.

If you find yourself getting nervous or distracted, take a couple of deep breaths or drink some water. Paraphrasing what your subject just said can help both of you focus. It can also help them clarify their points. Sometimes you'll want to use this method to allow them to have the most developed version of their thoughts and the simplest phrasing. This makes for the best quotes.

Whether you are recording using magnetic tape or a digital medium (more on this below) be sure to bring enough, and then some. It would be a shame to run out once you get your subject on a roll and the interview takes an extra twenty minutes.

If you are taking photos, be sure to have enough space in your camera. Test the flash in this environment before taking photos. Bring extra batteries for your tape recorder and camera.

Try talking about other things. Sometimes the best material comes from discussing things that have nothing directly to do with your subject's vocation or main interest: upbringing, hobbies, popular music and TV shows. By straying from the beaten path, you may help to portray a warmer, more thoughtful side of a personality than most readers have seen.

Some zines, like *Slave to the Needles,* interview popular indie rockers, but only ask them questions about their knitting and related crafts. It definitely creates unique interviews that will not be replicated elsewhere.

Keep in touch with your interviewee. Send a thank-you note and a copy of the issue(s) that the interview appears in. Most likely, they will remember you, since many interviewers do *not* bother to follow up. This will help you maintain a good relationship, should you decide to interview the subject again down the line.

Your method will depend on your personal style, your typing ability, and other variables. Some people really are more comfortable with just taking notes, and if you're one of them, that is fine. In some cases, the subject may even prefer that you use a pen and pad. Still, unless you know speedwriting or some other form of shorthand, it's difficult to scribble notes while you are trying to keep up with a stream of dialog. People speak much faster than they write. Generally, most people write at about 30 words per minute, type from 40 to 120 words per minute, and speak at over 200 words per minute. A recorder saves you the burden of having to split your focus.

Recorders

A recorder avoids the risk of missing something great (and sometimes you can only tell it's great during playback; I'm always amazed at what I miss during the actual encounter). It's also protection in case someone contests a quote you use.

If you use a recorder, test it out in an environment that approximates that of the interview. Use decent equipment, even if you have to borrow it. A small digital or cassette recorder with a condenser (omni-directional) mic may be fine, or you may need better equipment and a directional mic. In any case, try to get a quiet setting for the interview; it eliminates background noise. A cheap recorder taping someone in a noisy diner is probably not going to get good results. The worst thing that could happen would be to lose the interview because your equipment was inadequate, or the background was too noisy.

HINT: If you use tape, it's a good idea to label the tape or tapes with the subject's name and the date of the interview; you might want to state those things at the beginning of your tape as well.

HINT: If you use a digital recorder, make a backup of the file ASAP to avoid the possibility of overwriting. Be sure to use a setting on your recorder that maximizes the quality and maximizes the amount of time you have to tape the interview. Again, always allow for the interview to run over the allotted time.

Set the counter to zero before you begin. You can easily find the highlights later by jotting down topics and numbers. If the subject talks about one thing at #345 on the counter, then another at #657, you can just write down the number on a pad.

Example:
#345 describes first sexual experience
#657 joined the circus

Phone Interviews
If you have an answering machine with recording capability, then you have an easy way to tape a phone interview. Some localities *require* that you tell your subject that you are recording the conversation; if your machine is silent, it's probably a good idea to make a statement to that effect just after you start the recorder. There are simple instructions for a phone patch recorder in the book Making Stuff and Doing Things.

E-Mail Interviews
This may work best if your subject is very busy or this is the only way to get an interview. There are several limitations with this format. Such interviews lack the give-and-take that makes face-to-face or phone interviews conversational. It's easy to spot them on the page; people write differently than they speak. Also, it may be difficult to get clarification on a point that could be easily explained in person. It can also mean that you lose control over your interview; for instance, you are dependent upon them to send back responses in a timely fashion, and if they skip a question, there's no easy way to get them to answer it.

On the positive side, however, it is easy to construct a concise interview that avoids rambling, and requires no transcribing. Depending upon your mutual resources, you can use the mail, a fax machine, or email to communicate at pretty much any hour of the day or night, regardless of time zones. Online chat rooms – can provide a good solution for multi-party interviews, and you will already have a rough transcript to develop from, once the interview is over.

Transcribing The Interview

You will have to somehow make your interview tidy enough to publish. If you handwrite your zine, then it's a matter of editing and writing out the pertinent parts neatly enough to read.

Most people dislike doing transcription, as it is long, involved, and arduous. If you record your interviews, then I highly recommend getting a transcription machine. These are the devices that people use to dictate letters and such to their secretarial staff. They are better paced for recording and playback. They are absolutely ideal for transcribing interviews. If you have to interrupt your typing every few words to click a tape recorder off and on, it will really slow you down. It's like the difference between a limousine and a city bus in terms of both speed and comfort.

Search for them in used office furniture stores (the Yellow Pages is good for that), or, cheapest of all, in junk shops, thrift stores, eBay, Craigslist, and the like. Most companies have chucked their old dictation machines by now, but if you or someone you know works for a large company, ask if they have any in storage – they'll probably just give the thing to you. Be sure that the format of the machine matches the format of your tapes, though. There are three formats: standard cassette, micro cassette, and even an antiquated minicassette format, which is useless unless you also have access to a stash of the right size tapes.

When Enough Is Too Much

One final note: I have always ended up with extra material. Interviews almost always contain more material than you should publish. Edit, edit, edit. Respect your readers' time and attention span. You can always spread a really engrossing interview across two issues or more. It gives readers a reason to come back. Focus on the parts that are most interesting to you, and your readers will most likely enjoy what you print.

diy comix
By Fly

A lot of artists have self-published before becoming recognized and getting deals with established publishers. Some recent examples are Julie Doucet, Adrian Tomine, Peter Kuper, and Eric Drooker. A lot of the underground cartoonists of the '60s put out their own magazines and created a sort of revolution within the comics industry. R. Crumb put together a comic with his brother when they were just kids. Jerry Seigel (creator of Superman) put out his first fanzine in 1929 called *Cosmic Stories*. This was one of the first of a wave of science fiction fan publications. For an insightful and fact-filled background on the history of comics, I recommend reading <u>Men of Tomorrow</u> by Gerard Jones, published by Basic Books.

Story Ideas & Scripting
A lot of DIY comix are based on personal stories, but this doesn't have to be the case. You can create a story based on fact or fiction or any mix of the two. Sometimes you might want to tell a story based on a true event but change the characters slightly so as not to embarrass, incriminate, or otherwise expose real individuals. You may want to change the sequence or details of events in order to allow the story to flow better. You may want to write a story where you are the main character, but you don't want

it to be so personal, so you change the "I" character to a third person character. For example, I do a series of comics based on a "fictional" character called K9. The stories depicted are based on real-life events that I experienced but I have changed some details of the story so it would all make sense without going into too many personal details. I feel that if I was representing it as "absolute truth," I would have to be more conscious of following the facts to the letter. In this case I didn't want to be tied down to all the details and complications that this would entail.

At one point, I did a comic about my first 24 hours in NYC back in 1988. I used a character, the Goddess Garbage, to represent myself. I also had another character who was based on a real person, and although I didn't use his actual name, he visually resembled the real guy. The comic had lots of funny details about rough squats and piss buckets and junkies having fits. It was published in the *New York Press*, the guy saw it, and recognized himself immediately, and he got so pissed off at me! He used to yell at me on the street for years after that. I'm telling you this to illustrate what can happen when you put real-life characters into your comics. They might not always like how they're portrayed.

There are cases where following the facts to the letter is an integral part of the story. Some political comics, like Joe Sacco's <u>Palestine</u> and <u>Safe Area Gorazde</u>, – both

A Fly comic about cement-mixing that needed to be accurate.

deal with exposing the real-life political situation and personal conflicts within war zones. Sacco is a journalist as well as a comics artist, and his work is informative, educational and necessary. Seth Tobocman's work is another example of political comics that work to convey real-world situations. His book <u>War in the Neighborhood</u> recounts the conflict between squatters and real estate development sympathizers in the Lower East Side of NYC. His work is his own personal story of involvement as an activist in the struggle for housing. Tobocman is also a co-founder of the *World War 3 Illustrated,* which is an example of collective self publishing – a collection of work by political cartoonists, writers, and illustrators that has been coming out since approximately 1980.

Another interesting place to get ideas for stories is from your dreams. It can be very useful and inspirational to keep a dream journal, though it can be difficult to write while you are still half-asleep. If you keep a notebook and pen by your bed, you can train yourself to jot down notes immediately upon waking or even in the middle of the night. I have done several comics based entirely on dreams (with a little tweaking to make it flow into a "story"). They make great stories even if they are a little abstract.

Scripting

There are a lot of different approaches to scripting. If you want to learn the DC method of story writing and scripting, a good reference book is <u>The DC Comics Guide to Writing Comics</u> by Dennis O'Neil. Although he is dealing mainly with the idea of writing superhero comics, he has some very good points on plot and character development and reprints examples of different approaches to scripting, from simple notes to detailed, page by page, panel-by-panel breakdowns of narrative, dialog and descriptions of action. Such detailed scripts might be provided when a writer and artist are working together yet independently on a project. In the "Industry" it is common to have the writer, editor, penciller, inker, colorist, and letterer be different people.

Starting

Dennis O'Neil has some good tips about comic story writing. He recommends that you know the end of the story before you write the beginning. He divides the story structure into 3 acts: Act 1 is the "hook", *an inciting incident that establishes the situation and conflict.* This action could also be translated visually as a "splash" page, *a full page of visual action to introduce the reader to the story and excite their interest.* Act 2 is the meat of your story, the development and complication of situations. Act 3 is the events leading to a climax. Then comes the denouement, the winding up, or resolution of the story.

- The plot and sub-plots are the action of the story advancing toward a resolution
- Character development supports the plot – you might have a hero and an anti-hero (or antagonist) and other supporting characters

- Think of the motivations of your character:
- What does he/she want?
- What or who does he/she love?
- What is he/she afraid of?
- Why does he/she involve him/herself in situations?

All of these points are not hard and fast rules, but they are useful to keep in mind in order to keep a focus to your story. What are you trying to communicate? You might want to write a personal story like a journal or a recounting of a specific event. In that case, the way the story tells itself is often similar to the approach O'Neil describes in creating fictional stories. There is usually some sort of protagonist and antagonist, resulting in some kind of conflict; exciting or interesting events unfold, and then there is a resolution.

To start, it is a good idea to keep it simple and to the point. Don't get sidetracked or bogged down by too many distracting details. You should focus on what is important to the story. It's useful to begin by outlining the main

Fly comics adapted from dreams.

events or "beats" of the story. This can help estimate the number of pages and possibilities for panel breakdowns. You can use Post-its or index cards or a computer at this stage. Once you get the basic plot laid out, you can use this as your outline and go straight to sketching out "thumbnails" (miniature versions of your page layout), or you could write a more detailed script.

My own personal version of scripting is extremely loose. Usually I have the story written. For example, my comic *Meanwhile* was based on a dream I had written down. I knew my page count, so I went through the story and divided the action into different pages and then started drawing. However, I have also worked on comics where someone else wrote the script. For example, I did a two-page comic about Mother Jones, and the script was written by Trina Robbins. Because the comic had to be as historically accurate as possible, I was thankful for her detailed panel-by-panel descriptions and directions.

But this project is all up to you. You are the writer, artist, publisher and distributor, so it's all about creating something that you care about and that is true to your vision. Finding & developing that vision is one of the simplest tenets of making a zine.

Thumbnails & Sketches
Once you have your story or script written and before you start sketching, there are some important things you need to know:
How many pages will you be working with?
What is the size or dimension of those pages?

Thumbnails
Once you figure out your dimensions and page count it's time to start considering how the story will be translated with art onto the page. Many artists do thumbnails at this point – *miniature versions of the page where you can experiment with different layout designs and panel configurations*. This may help you refine how your story will be broken down into separate pages. It can help you establish your pacing and sense of time and space.

Character Research
Before you start doing your sketches, it might be useful to do some preliminary work, especially if you are working on a story that is based on real events. Research of images and settings is very effective to create a sense of "realism". Even if your art is not "realistic", if it is based on actual research you might be able to create a more convincing imaginary reality. Of course your story might be based purely on fantasy. Even so, if you can practice drawing from life it will help you manipulate your images in a way that you might be better able to communicate your story without the art becoming too confusing or

unrecognizable. For example, I did a comic based on a dream that I had where I crossed a bridge. Although it was a dream sequence and all the lines were warped, I based the images on some sketches I had done of bridges.

Character Design

It can also be very beneficial to do some preliminary sketches to develop your characters. This can help you practice drawing your characters from all angles and still keep them consistent and consistency will help your readers to follow the story. If one character looks different in every panel then it will become confusing. Similarly if all of your characters look the same it will be hard to follow the story. Developing the character is very important in stories that are based on real people. For example, in Seth Tobocman's comic about Mumia Abu Jamal, an African-American journalist unjustly on death row for several decades, it was essential that Tobocman study Mumia and practice drawing him before doing the comic. Anything less may have undermined the importance of the story.

If you work on your character development, you will be more confident when it comes to putting the final sketches together and this will help you communicate more effectively to your readers. Even if you are doing very cartoony and simplified drawings, it helps to practice drawing from life. It will help you in making your characters more animated and relatable to the reader.

Page Design

To me, this is one of the hardest steps – starting to visualize your story – there are just so many possibilities! It's up to you to create your own visual vocabulary and present it within a believable sense of time and space.

A few components to keep in mind are:
Clarity (what is the point or focus of your story?)
Realism (not necessarily "realistic" art but a sense of credibility. Can the reader believe in your "world"?)
Dynamism (keeping it interesting and full of life)
Continuity (backgrounds, character appearance, "axis of action" or direction of action and "props").

Deciding what to illustrate and what to break down into dialog and how to compose it all so it works fluidly is a skill that will develop with experience. You can use your intuition to great effect during this process to figure out what works and what doesn't. What kind of images and in what order do you need to get your story across? What should you illustrate, what should be conveyed in dialogue, and what should be a caption? It might be superfluous to write a caption saying "he walked upstairs" and then have a picture of a guy walking upstairs. There are many different ways to combine words and images to create a comic.

Scott McCloud breaks it down in his book <u>Understanding Comics</u> as follows:
Word specific – images illustrate text
Picture specific – mainly visual sequence
Duo specific – both image and text in equal balance
Additive – words amplify or elaborate image (or vice versa)
Parallel – words and image follow different tracks simultaneously
Montage – like collage – words as visual element
Interdependent –

(this is the most commonly used approach in comics) – words and pictures work together to convey an idea that neither could convey alone

Remember in setting up any page that people in the western world generally read a page from left to right and top to bottom. If your panels are arranged to flow in any other odd configuration, make sure that this is clear, or you could end up confusing your reader and distracting them from the story.

As you figure out your page layout, keep in mind a sense of timing. Using a grid pattern of panels (all equal size) can somewhat neutralize the reader's sense of time passing. Using different shapes and configurations of panels can reinforce the sense of time and space. For example a stretched-out panel might indicate more time passing or create a sense of more space. A panel containing an inset panel with a close-up might indicate an almost instantaneous action. You can also affect the sense of timing with the space in between panels. The panels should work coherently together to move your story forward.

Scott McCloud defines this idea as "closure", "the phenomenon of observing the parts but perceiving the whole." I recommend taking a look at his book <u>Understanding Comics</u> for an in-depth discussion of the concept of the panel and how to use it. Another great reference book is Will Eisner's <u>Comics & Sequential Art</u>. Eisner was a master storyteller and much of his compositional work is pure genius.

Some points he makes about using panels are:

Panel borders – need not always be straight lines. They can be used to indicate flashbacks or dreams; for example, they could also indicate emotional content. Jagged edges may give the feeling of danger or agitation. The lack of borders may indicate a sense of unlimited space and may give the audience the opportunity to create the background with their imaginations.

Framing – the panel borders could become a structural element of the story, for example, a doorway or a window.

Panel composition – when considering your panel composition, keep in mind the focus point and consider continuity with other panels. Establish a sense of perspective and then embellish.

experimental panels broken up by speech that create a very spastic and hectic effect.

Perspective within the panel can manipulate the reader's orientation and affect emotional states as well as conveying information. An overhead view may give the reader a feeling of being more detached. Eye level views may let the audience feel more involved and make the action seem more immediate. A ground level view might create more of a sense of vulnerability in the reader.

However you arrange your panels and create your compositions, try to keep in mind the information and emotion you are trying to convey – is it relevant to your story? Is it moving your story forward in a coherent and interesting way?

Klaus Janson's book <u>The DC Comics Guide to Penciling Comics</u> details all the steps and considerations involved in creating comics art from a script. When structuring pages and panels he recommends considering:

Eye Movement—more eye movement might create more excitement and interest. Is your focal point in the center of every panel or are you moving it around?
Contrast—contrast of shapes and sizes as well as black and white) Balance (symmetrical or asymmetrical?
The Diagonal—designing the action or the figures on diagonals can add a more dynamic feeling and create more depth.

Janson goes on to describe the different kinds of "shots and angles" that are effectively used in comics:
Establishing shot – often at the beginning to establish the setting.
Extreme long shot – for example, a cityscape. It could also be used as an establishing shot.
Long shot – characters may be visible but do not dominate the setting.
Full shot – full length of body shown with the background secondary to characters.
Medium shot – maybe about half the body of the character. Background is simplified or non-existent.
Close-up – character from the top of the shoulders to the top of the head. Background is simplified or nonexistent.
Extreme close-up – character's face or part of the face fills the panel. Brings the reader right into the action.

It's a good idea to use variety depending on the needs of your story. The information and emotion you are trying to convey should affect the focus, perspective and composition of your panels. Remember to try to keep it directionally consistent. If your character is facing or moving in a certain direction in one panel, make sure you maintain that orientation in the following panel. If you mix it up you might end up confusing your reader.

My Comix Experience

When I first started making comix, I tried to make each page like a painting with all the action flowing together – I had no concept of "panels". I usually didn't plan out my pages (except in my head). I would just start drawing. This worked sometimes, but sometimes it didn't. As I continued drawing comix I became better at actually planning a page and I even used panels! I would also do some preliminary sketches of the places I was trying to depict. Eventually I started working on comix that were based on real events and to me the details of the story were very important, as well as the images. I was using a lot of words. Some of the aspects of the stories were really intense. For example, incidents of physical and sexual abuse. I didn't want to make it harder for the reader to ingest the story, so I tried to arrange things in a straightforward, very legible way. I didn't want to trivialize the content by making the compositions too "arty" or hard to read. I found using actual panels more efficient in getting my point across.

Usually I skip the thumbnail stage, but I do rough sketches at full size to figure out my page layout and what text I will include. Then I will sometimes lay out the panels with the captions on the computer in Quark. Then I print out the pages and do the final sketches on the printouts. But I don't always use the computer to lay out the pages. Sometimes I will just draw the whole thing freehand, especially if I

*an establishing shot from Fly's **K-9's First Time:The Boyfriend***

an extreme close up shot from the same story

am including unusual panel shapes. After that, I transfer the sketches onto a light, smooth Bristol. These would be my final pencils. The next step would be inking.

It's a good idea to always carry a sketchbook with you, even a small one. You never know when you will see a person or a place that will either inspire you to create a new character or setting, or help you work on developing your current ideas. Many times you will see something or think of something and you'll think it's so obvious that you will remember it, but then later it's gone! Tragedy!!

Final Art & Inking:

Figure out the process you want to use in going from your rough sketches to final art and inking. It's good to keep a few things in mind. Make sure that all your dimensions and page counts are correct. If you've made a mistake, now is the time to catch it. Once you're happy with your sketches you could ink directly on your drawings, however there are several disadvantages to this. Rough sketches tend to be just that, rough, with lots of pencil lines. Therefore it might be hard to erase after inking. The ink could smear, the paper could rip and some of the pencil lines may be so dark that they show up in the printing process.

Final Pencils

The advantage of doing a stage of final pencils is that you can clean everything up. This might be essential if someone else will be doing the inking stage. You can also put your final pencils on better paper. I use a smooth, light Bristol board, which will make them more durable.

When I first started doing comix I used pens and inked directly on my first sketches. This method works but I found as I continued doing comix that it was better to do a stage of finished pencils from the sketches. It improved the drawing. I was able to refine it and the difference was noticeable. Also, if you want to keep your originals in good condition. Maybe to reprint them at a later date or to show or sell them – they age better if you put them on better paper.

I also stopped using pens for the most part and ink mainly with a brush and Sumi ink. I found that using a brush and ink gave me a cleaner, more tapered line (the pen line always seems a little fuzzy to me). Also, it allowed more fluidity. I felt it easier to get a sense of movement within the drawing by using the brush.

Usually I transfer my rough sketches to the Bristol using a light table. If you don't have access to a light table, you can tape your original sketch up to a window during the day and tape the Bristol over that, and you have a natural light table. Another option is to get a piece of Plexiglas and put it over a milk crate with a clamp light beneath it. This works ok except that the light heats up the plexi and makes it a little warped. I usually wear a cotton glove on my drawing hand so that I don't get hand grease on the paper. I have had problems in the past with the ink refusing to adhere properly to the paper, and I thought it might be because of greasiness, but a lot of people don't seem to have this problem.

The size you do your final art is up to you, as long as the dimensions are correct. I used to try to do all my final art a little bigger than the print size would be. Often the art looks better and tighter when you reduce it. But you also have to consider your production techniques. Will you be scanning your art? If it's too big and won't fit on the scanner, then you will have to scan it in sections and stitch it together in Photoshop. These days, I try to work in a format that will fit my scanner, so I don't have to do that (though sometimes it's unavoidable). I usually work either at 100% or slightly larger (if the print size is smaller than 8.5"x11")

Inking
There are various methods and approaches to inking final art. Making DIY comix is a good opportunity to experiment with different materials and styles. The mood and content of your story can also be an indicator for how you will approach inking it. If your art is very geometric, then a Rapidograph pen might be a good option for you. If you want a dark engraved look, then you might want to try scratchboard. To achieve a more painterly and fluid line, you could use a brush. Of course, all of these mediums are capable of expressing a wide range of emotions and ideas in how you use them. You can also combine methods. It's a good idea to check out other comix and see how other artists have approached similar materials.

Some of the more popular inking techniques include
Disposable pens
Brush pens
Rapidograph pens
Crow quill pens
Brush and ink
Scratch board (comes in black or white)

I have also done final artwork using watercolor pencils and collage and ink together. This looked great when it was printed in a glossy magazine, but it didn't work so well when I included it in a photocopied zine. You always have to be aware of your production method as you are deciding what materials to use. If you are using washes or tones, I recommend scanning your originals and doing your layout on the computer, so that you don't have to deal with copies of copies when you produce your zine. For a photocopied zine, I have found that straight black and white is the easiest to work with and gives the best results.

Paste Up and Production

Since you are working on photocopied zines, you have to keep in mind the limitations and abilities of a photocopier when you are preparing your work. You are limited to copying on 8.5x11 or 8.5x14 or 11x17 size paper – if you want your zine to be a different size, you will have to trim it after it has been copied.

If your originals are larger than the size of your masters, then you could reduce them on a photocopier, or scan them and print them at a reduced size. Of course, if you are doing all of your layout on the computer, you will have to scan all of your artwork. If your art is line art, you can easily use photocopy reductions to do your paste up, but if you have used gray tones in your originals, you should probably scan them and print them out as halftones, as these will photocopy much better. If your originals are the same size as your masters will be, you could photocopy straight from them. You just have to make sure the layout is in the correct order.

Recommended reading:

Understanding Comics by Scott McCloud—published by Kitchen Sink
Comics & Sequential Art by Will Eisner published by Poorhouse Press
Graphic Storytelling and Visual Narrative by Will Eisner published by Poorhouse Press
The DC Comics Guide to Writing Comics by Dennis O'Neil published by Watson-Guptill
Men of Tomorrow (a history of comics) by Gerard Jones published by Basic Books
Writing for Comics with Peter David published by Impact
The DC Comics Guide to Penciling Comics by Klaus Janson published by Watson & Guptill
The Art of Comic Book Inking – vol. 1 & 2 by Gary Martin published by Dark Horse
The DC Comics Guide to Penciling Comics by Klaus Janson published by Watson & Guptill

I Would Recommend Reading Comics By

Seth Tobocman, Joe Sacco, Eric Drooker, Peter Kuper, Will Eisner, Mary Fleener, Kim Deitch, Sabrina Jones, Megan Kelso, Abby Denson, Sophie Crumb, Alexandar Zograf, Mac McGill, Art Spiegelman, Windsor McKay, Cristy Road, Liz Baillie, Dori Seda, Gabrielle Bell, Jennifer Camper, The Hernandez Brothers, Peter Bagge, Gary Panter, Charles Burns, Dan Clowes, Moebius, Marjane Satrapi, Fiona Smyth, Carel Moiseiwitsch, Phoebe Glockner, Carrie McNinch, Aline Kominsky-Crumb, Leslie Sternbergh, Nicole Shulman, Trina Robbins (has written several books on the history of women in comics), Howard Cruse, Sue Coe

contributors

When I published my zine, I used multiple contributors for each issue. I sent every contributor their guidelines and ensured they understood them before publishing their first piece. This way, people were clear of what was expected and what they would receive. No contributor ever complained that I misrepresented what my zine was or what I would do with their work.

Treat contributors with respect. Get them copies of the zine before anyone else, if possible. A thank-you note is a nice touch. Try to maintain an ongoing relationship. This is also a good time to let them know about upcoming timelines, while they're still excited about seeing their work in your zine. If you nurture your relationship, they will want to work with you again and again. As long as contributors feel you take their work and your zine seriously, you will never have a shortage of submissions.

Submissions come in every form imaginable. E-mail attachments (or text pasted right into an email) are the simplest because they don't require retyping. Specify text formats and program versions to ensure compatibility with your equipment. Rich Text Format ("RTF") seems to open most easily across the greatest range of platforms and software. Avoid experimenting with encoding, compression, or unusual formats when you're on a deadline and don't have time to work through glitches.

Sometimes things don't work out. A contributor could be difficult or demanding to work with; someone could beg for deadline extensions and then stand you up. These things can happen under the best of circumstances. Don't hold a grudge. You should acknowledge that, unless you are paying $50 or more per item, you are essentially relying on volunteer labor. What you can offer is a small degree of prestige (more if the zine is widely known and respected). It is also very satisfying for most contributors to see their work in print, but be realistic. Don't expect from others the same degree of slavish devotion to your project that you may feel.

On the other hand, don't be a doormat. You deserve to be taken seriously. If a contributor is flaky, cut your losses and move on. There are plenty of creative folks out there who'd like to see their work appear in zines.

Do I Pay Contributors?
Some zines do, but most don't, mostly due to lack of funds. In lieu of payment, you can barter ad space for submissions or extra copies of the zine. It's nice a way of acknowledging contributors when money is scarce. You can barter for fun things like cookies, haircuts, dinner, handmade crafts, or anything that respects the time and effort put into the submission.

If you can afford to pay a little, great. If you can't, be up-front about this from the beginning. A lot of folks in the zine world regard financial considerations as a necessary complication. Depending on your available pool of contributors, you may need to pay a bit because without any visuals a zine can look pretty dull, no matter how good the writing is.

How Do I Find Contributors?
If you know other writers, that's the obvious place to start. Friends and family are another. Sometimes the best material comes from people who claim they're not writers. You never know.

Look for work you like by people in other zines, and then contact them. Usually a polite, friendly note to the editor is all that's needed.

If you really want a broad base of people from your community involved or are having trouble finding writers, you could post notices at colleges, grocery stores, libraries, or anywhere with a corkboard. Any place where there are creative people has some possible contributors. You can post notices on Internet user groups or interest-specific websites looking for contributors as well.

Once people know you are doing a zine, they will approach you. Have a set of creative guidelines ready to give out when they do.

As a last resort, you could, in theory, list your zine in publications like *Writer's Market*, *Fiction Writer's Market*, *Poet's Market*, and *Artist's Market*. These are all widely available in bookstores. The problem with these resources is that you may be deluged by lots of unwanted submissions by folks who've never seen your zine and have no idea what you're about. They will typically just submit whatever finished work they have and it is typically pretty self-indulgent. Specify that folks should read your zine before submitting their work.

If you're doing a genre-specific publication like sci-fi, mystery, or horror, there are professional associations for most genres, and at least one newsletter that lists calls for submission.

Rejections

Pretty much however you manage your zine, you'll get submissions you don't want to print, and will need to notify these people with some kind of a response. Set aside time to answer submissions, whether you do each one as it arrives, or let them pile up for a week or a month.

I think that if you can scribble a line or two on a letter, even a form letter, it personalizes and energizes your correspondence. Enclose weird/funny postcards, flyers for your projects, photos, and other fun or strange material. Try offering one or two simple, constructive suggestions. It's not your job to make someone a good writer or artist, just to respond in a courteous manner.

Some people just don't send rejections and ignore things they won't print. This can be confusing to the person submitting, but I can understand the inclination not to engage in a possibly heady dialogue where feelings are likely to be hurt. People are often submitting things that are very personal to them and sometimes quite emotional.

HINT: Try to keep your rejection letters personal, because nobody like a form letter. Include information on anything you're up to.

What If My Project Doesn't Happen?
While it's embarrassing to tell contributors that you've canceled your project, it's more embarrassing when they call, email, or run into you on the street and ask what happened. Return their work with an explanatory note, thanking them for their time and effort. This should stand you in good stead should you decide you want their work for another project later.

fn 1 Writer's Digest Books, 4700 E Galbraith Rd Cincinnati, OH 45236 (513) 531-2222. www.writersdigest.com

inspiration and creativity

In our experience, most people are quite understanding when it comes to delays. On the other hand, it's somehow acceptable in the zine world to delay for years, which gives all of us a bad name. Be consistent; even if you only publish a new issue every year or three. Stay in touch with the people invested in your zine, especially if there's a legitimate cause for the delay.

Everything in the zine world is tentative and subject to change but don't make promises you can't keep. As long as you don't sabotage your reputation, most people remain remarkably trusting and understanding.

STRESS—Energy held without release; tension.

Reducing Stress
Make a list of things that are causing you stress. Are there tasks you can delegate? For instance, maybe you can get a friend to help you sell ads, review other zines, or fill orders.

Are there things you can eliminate from your process? Let's say you have a bin of unsolicited manuscripts, which you may consider sending back, unread, to the writers because your publication schedule is full right now. Reading this kind of mail always ends up on the bottom of my list because it is really time-consuming to read. Compose a thoughtful response, and mail the thing out. Sometimes it's kinder to return these unread with a brief, form-letter explanation than to hold onto them for months and months with no acknowledgment at all, in the unlikely hope that your schedule will change.

Eliminate anything that is draining your energy and embrace the tasks that you love. Create ways to spend more of your time on them. Similarly, every time you think about that bin of mail, the distraction is draining a bit of your energy and focus. The sooner you can deal with it, the sooner you will clear that space in your head to pay more attention to the things you enjoy.

Here are a few simple techniques for reducing stress:

Focus on the here and now. Stop what you are doing and just sit still for a few minutes. Make yourself comfortable. Empty your mind of cares and worries. Every time you have a stressful thought, acknowledge it and let it go. Just do your best in the present, and trust that the future will take care of itself. You are actually acknowledging that your peace of mind is more important than an arbitrary time crunch. This simple meditation can be very helpful, and the more you do it, the easier it gets.

Do something physical to relieve tension. Let your hands drop to your sides. Close your eyes. Take a few deep breaths, inhaling through the nose and exhaling through your mouth. Massage your eyes and face with your fingers. Roll your eyes around, or alternate opening them wide and closing them tight a few times. Shake out your hands and relax your shoulders.

Take a break. Stand up. Stretch. Walk down the hall. Get a glass of water. Have a snack. Go outside. Walk around the block. Stretch some more. Sometimes simple stretches like head rolls, shoulder shrugs, twisting at the waist, reaching for the sky, and reaching for your toes can do wonders to relieve crankiness.

Set a time limit and stick to it. Agree to work on the zine for, say, the next two hours, and then do something else, preferably a reward for all the hard work you've just done on the zine. You do not do your best work when you are tired. Something that works for me is alternating two hours of "work" with an hour or two of something fun.

Drink fluids. When you're hard at work, it's easy to forget to drink enough liquid. I find it helps to drink lots of water or herbal tea, so I always have a glass or mug around. Most tension headaches are related to dehydration. Coffee and beer tend to dehydrate you.

If you're working at a computer, dehydration is an even bigger problem. Studies have proven that people blink less when they are working at a computer screen; which causes the eyes to dry out. The longer you work in front of a screen, the worse it gets. That's one reason for taking breaks and setting time limits. An anti-glare screen can relieve a lot of eye stress.

Change your visual focus. Whether you are working at a computer, a paste-up table, or a copier, look up periodically and focus on something in the distance for a minute. Look around at different things. This is good to do when you're taking a break. Refocusing relieves pressure on your eye muscles, which tend to tense up when you are doing close-up work. Changing where your work area is located can also have a startling affect on your productivity.

Take off your shoes and loosen your clothes. I'm more comfortable and relaxed when I'm working in slippers or socks and loose clothing.

Inspiration

Inspiration is the impulse to do creative work. There is an excitement, a feeling of "A-ha!", and sometimes the feeling that you are being pushed by an unknown force to accomplish a goal.

It's more likely inspiration comes to you when you are receptive to it. Some people draw inspiration from quiet settings, whereas others get inspired by the adrenaline rush of a busy setting, like seeing tons of other people's work at a conference or festival. Any event that engages your full attention and stimulates one or more of the senses can be inspirational. This is often a profound or deeply emotional experience. You can help it along by placing yourself in settings that inspire you. Sometimes it's a great movie or great rock show. Some find inspiration from hanging out with their latest crush or spending personal time with someone else who is productive or engaging. Others derive inspiration from nature, a long bicycle ride, or taking a workshop. Literature of any kind, especially other people's zines, can be very inspirational. Sometimes you just have a great idea, and who knows where it came from.

One of the unique qualities of zines is that they are usually based in, and fueled by inspiration. You have to be inspired enough to publish a document about a particular person, hobby, movement, or worldview. Sometimes that inspiration is fleeting and the zine is short-lived. In other cases, it can become the basis of a literary career.

Where Does Creativity Come From?

If inspiration is the impulse to make something, then creativity is the act itself.

So much creativity is the accumulation of developed ideas. Learning to nurture these thoughts and process them becomes easier over time. You can store your ideas mentally, but it's also useful to keep a folder or notebook to collect your constant brainstorms. Forgetting a great idea is the worst!

Give your ideas a chance to develop; we're our own worst critics. That's why an idea folder works so well; it gives us a place to hide things until we're really ready to see how they work together.

The world makes room for, and nurtures, our creative impulse. Anyone who puts out more than a couple issues of a zine is bound to improve simply because they have the opportunity to make refinements to their original concept. With anything, you will improve through practice.

HINT: The important thing is to simply write — anything. One technique is to sit with a pen and pad (or at a keyboard) and to keep writing for a predetermined length of time: 5 minutes, 15 minutes, whatever. You can use a clock, a kitchen timer or the alarm on a digital watch. The only condition of this exercise is that you cannot stop writing or typing. It's okay to write gibberish, to repeat yourself, to type your thoughts as you're having them, your fantasies, anything—just as long as you keep writing. Often this technique can trigger an idea or help you work through a creative block. Most of it will probably be useless, but surprisingly often, this technique inspires at least one useful phrase, thought, or idea.

So go to it, and good luck!

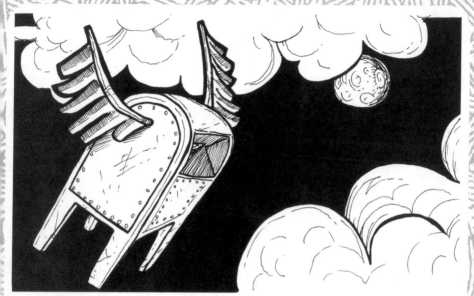

postage

Nurture a positive relationship with your postal workers! This will help more than you can imagine in a year or two. It's a good bet that your post-person will be a lot more understanding when problems arise if you've taken the time to develop a personal relationship.

Priority Mail
The post office has created some flat-rate volume-based envelopes and boxes in response to the vast number of people who do shipping because of Ebay. This is to your advantage since priority mail envelopes and boxes are relatively cheap, especially compared to normal priority mail rates. They can also contain a lot of zines, and normally arrive in 2-3 days. They are not guaranteed however, and can sometimes arrive up to 30 days later.

Media Mail
Media mail must contain "books", which are defined as "8 or more pages bound together, that do not contain advertisements", and also "film, printed music, test materials, sound recordings (CD, cassette, record, etc), binders of medical information, and computer-readable media."

At six ounces or less, Media Mail and First Class rates are basically the same. If your package weighs more than seven ounces, it becomes cheaper (albeit slower) to use Media Mail.

Once your package is a few pounds or more, media mail becomes vastly cheaper and if you are mailing numerous media packages of a few pounds, you'll quickly be saving lots of cash. With Media Mail, you pay a flat fee for the first pound, and subsequent pounds are even cheaper. This is a very economical way to ship multiple copies of your zine to a store, distributor, or any other place that you wish to ship to in bulk quantity. Go to usps.gov for current rates.

The Postal Service will sometimes refuse to let you use Media Mail to send zines, but the distinction between a "pamphlet" and a "book" is mostly arbitrary. The policy on Media Mail seems inconsistent and varies from branch to branch. Your best defense is to know the fine print, "But ma'am, this is a book over 8 pages, bound, with no paid advertising. It contains no correspondance."

International Mail

Your options are a little bit different here but the concept is the same. The cheapest options are generally the global flat rate envelopes and boxes, unless you are mailing something 5 ounces or less. Flat rate envelopes are slow and expensive to Canada and some countries, like Italy and Nigeria, do not accept them. Otherwise, they are fast, efficient, and relatively cheap. A 9x12" envelope costs about $10. Exact rates change frequently. You'll need to fill out a little green customs form including what is inside your package and the value. Zines are best described as pamphlets for the postal staff's understanding. The United Kingdom and Canada both have pretty fierce taxes on imported paper, so it's often best to keep the stated value per package as low as possible.

The first questions here are usually: What's a good price to charge? Where are the stores or distributors that will carry your zine, and how do you approach them? What are other ways of disseminating your zine? How do you get subscribers?

Pricing and Budget

One of the best things about zines is their affordability. In many cases, for one to five dollars, you can get a solid evening's entertainment. So how do you price your zine? Look at other zines and see what they're charging. If your zine is printed on nice paper, you can charge more than if it's on newsprint. The appearance of your cover contributes heavily to your publication's perceived value, especially in stores.

Your audience may be a factor as well. Readers of a zine on California wines probably have more to spend than flea market fans, but you never know; and longevity matters, too. A once obscure, now-popular zine could raise its cover price, but rarely does, unless necessary. Increasing page count, a screen-printed cover, labor-intensive packaging, adding color, or other obvious improvements justify raising the price.

Content matters, but so does form. If you offer thought-provoking material that's well laid out, with decently typewritten or typeset pages and great graphics, you can sell more copies than something similar which is poorly written, sloppily scrawled, and lacks visuals. If it tells a good story, or if it makes people laugh, that's a *big* plus.

One rule of thumb is to make your cover price three to six times what it costs you to produce a single copy. In other words, if you spend $100 making 200 copies of your 24-page, 1/2 size (5.5x8.5") zine stapled twice on the fold, you could charge $1 to $3 per copy and be within a reasonable range. Presuming that you charged $2/copy, and sold those for full price, you'd need to sell 50 copies, or a fourth of your print run, to make back your cost. If you were selling through stores and distributors at 50/50 terms, you'd be getting $1 a copy, and you'd need to sell 100 copies, or half, to cover costs. You could give away the rest or save some to sell to future fans as back issues. If you sold more than that, you might want to save some money toward your next issue.

Zinesters tend to be overly optimistic in terms of projected sales. It's also easy (and tempting) to overlook expenses such as postage, phone calls, and supplies. If you want to know what the cost of your zine really is, I suggest making a budget.

Stores
It can be a scary and daunting task to approach a store with your zine. A fear of rejection for something so personal can scare most people out of even considering the prospect. Here are some tips and general guidelines that may help.

A store will generally want 40% of the cover price of your zine. That means you'll get 60%. Price your zine accordingly before you talk to the store and know your numbers. Find a price that isn't so high that people won't buy your zine but high enough that it is sustainable to print as many as you'd like to have available. Industry logic dictates 5-10 times the cost of printing is your retail price, but 1)zines are not part of an industry and 2)that tends to create a prohibitive cover price that will alienate the people in your community, who would be reading your zine otherwise. For instance, 10 x $1 worth of copies is $10 for an approximate 40 page zine.

Most stores will take somewhere between 2 and 20 copies of your zine at a time. A common number to start out with is 5, in order to judge how fast they will sell.

Some stores that typically sell zines are alternative bookstores, independent record stores, cool comic shops, clothing shops, DIY boutiques, infoshops, coffee shops, newsstands, candy shops, video stores, and specialized zine stores. Ask people you know who do zines in your area and they could probably direct you to some stores. There is also a list of stores to start with in the back of this book. Aaron Cometbus often extols the virtues of getting his zine sold somewhere that's never sold them before. Figure out the places in your town that *should* be selling zines. Drop by a few times and be friendly and chatty. Come back a few more times if they aren't yet interested. In most cases, stores that don't presently sell zines are the best place to sell yours, as it will be the most visible one! It will probably get prime counter placement.

Piercing parlors and head shops sell zines sometimes. Why not try *beauty* parlors and *pet* shops? Think of what your zine is about and see if a store that sells related materials is interested in your zine – especially if they don't sell any other zines. Anything with enough of a following to support a store probably has a zine as well, and that store is a place to sell it.

It's not always easy though. It requires a five second sales pitch with an explanation of the zine and its content. Often times they'll pick it up on the spot. I've also approached magazine shops and other places that have art or other types of products that stray more from the mainstream where it seemed like they would be interested in the prospect of zines.

To sell your zine through a store in a different city, send them a single copy for free with a self addressed stamped envelope and a note requesting that they consider selling it. You can call after a month or two but at this point it is up to the store. Be patient.

Sometimes, it can work best when sending zines out of town on consignment, to think of them as a donation. Sometimes the time spent trying to collect a few dollars can outweigh the time, effort, and stress of succeeding. Remember, the greatest joy is getting feedback from people reading your zine in those towns!

Check up on how your zines are selling approximately every 90 days and be patient. Rome wasn't built in a day. Your zines won't sell in a day either.

Stores will often be financially strapped, so be patient, but don't be afraid to remind them. Keep copies of your invoices, just in case. To generate an invoice, include all of your contact information, the date, quantities, titles, wholesale price, and totals. It makes things easier for the person writing your checks if you give them a clear and readable invoice with all of your information.

Most importantly, support the stores that sell your zines! Look at what else they sell. Odds are they have other things you'd be interested in besides your zine.

The latest copy of *Zine World* has a feedback section on experiences with various distros and shops in the back pages. Write to ZINE WORLD, c/o Jerianne, PO Box 330156, Murfreesboro TN 37133. $4 per issue.

The book-selling industry is extremely volatile. Stores and distributors come and go at an alarming rate, and practically no one will pay you if they are closing up shop. One clerk or buyer may be the sole "anchor" for zines at a particular store; if she goes, that may spell the end of the store's zine-friendly attitude. Similarly, DIY zine distros come and go at equally alarming rates and you'll probably be investigating who has quit and what has sprung up since your last issue was published.

HINT: Whenever possible, get the money up front. Cash is always better than consignment, mostly because it reduces everyone's paperwork. If you must deal on a consignment basis, caveat ziner: Get something signed by someone acknowledging the date, price, terms (are you asking 50% of the cover price? 60%?), and the number of copies you are leaving. *Put the receipt in a safe place. Now.* **Right** *now.*

The Sales Call
Many people in the zine community have a tedious and nervous relationship with money. Its use undermines the community nature of what zines represent, but unlike most jobs, you get to sell something you made yourself, something that you really believe in, and you can do what you want with the money.

Fear of selling is real. It can be very discouraging. Sometimes the store's buyer will be swamped and unable to speak with you. Sometimes they will only be available at really weird hours. Sometimes the person taking your message will be distracted and treat you brusquely. Sometimes you will get trapped in voice mail hell. Sometimes you will have to call back buyers half a dozen times before getting the sale. Sometimes they will lose your zine, or worse, quit, and you will have to start all over again.

Still, this is the worst stuff that can happen. Sometimes they're glad to hear from you and eager to place an order. Sometimes they may actually call *you* and ask when the next issue is out. Sometimes they call to say they're sold out and want more copies of the current issue. Sometimes they double their previous order. Sometimes they say how much they like your zine. Sometimes buyers become your friends.

HINT: If you're still freaked out about making calls, set a time limit and quit as soon as you've reached it. Don't stop making calls until the time is up.

If someone asks you to call back, then by all means call back. Be persistent; it works. Sometimes I think stores picked up my zine simply because they realized it was one way to stop the inquiries. Many stores are swamped and buyers stressed out. Sometimes people are just in a bad mood and thus treat you disrespectfully. Try to maintain an upbeat tone in your voice. If they are busy, or if you need to speak with someone else, ask about the best time to call or drop in. Try to get the name of the person you spoke with, and the name of the person who spends the money, and *write them down.* Put all the information you collect into one place.

Sometimes you'll have problems where people won't want to give out their names because of security culture. They won't want their name linked to the place where they are helping out because it could label them as a terrorist under the absurd definitions now provided by the PATRIOT Act. Accept this and move on.

After the First Sales Call
Once you have a buyer on the line, ask for a *standing order* for your zine. This means that they agree to take a certain number of each issue you publish when it comes out. (I recommend a minimum of five; it's usually not worth the trouble of dealing with fewer.) This usually works best after they've sold through a few issues. This helps predict a more accurate print run for your next issue; and more importantly, saves you the trouble of having to call every single time.

Some zinesters *like* to call every store for every issue. It's up to you. I recommend calling about halfway between issues, or just dropping by if that's possible, to see how your zine is selling. If the issue is sold out, or close to it, you can usually get the store to take another batch. Sometimes they may call you if your zine is sold out, but this is not usually the case. Initiative pays. They've got hundreds if not thousands of titles to keep track of, and you've got one. Who's more likely to call whom?

I know of folks who split 50/50 for getting payment up front, and you might want to try this tactic with some stores. Terms could be 60/40 for payment within 15 days of shipment ("net 15"). Realize that in most cases, "net 30" means that the store will really pay you in 60 days, 90 days, or even longer. A lot of stores won't pay you until your next issue comes out, and even then you often have to wait a bit.

Please bear in mind that people who start bookstores, just like those who start zines and distros, tend to do so because they are passionate about it and not usually because they went to business school. As with any other business, the rules are what you and the buyer agree to.

Consignment

Many stores won't pay upfront for zines and you'll have to sign a form that says you'll get paid when your zines sell. This is called consignment. Don't expect to be paid upfront—the money that a store makes from selling zines barely makes it worthwhile for the amount of time and paperwork required to price, display, and collect money for them. Stores that sell zines generally do so because they *want* to and care about zine culture.

Whether you want to do consignment with stores is up to you. Typically, stores who want consignment basis are the smallest, they take the smallest amount, and are among the hardest to collect from. It's a lot of work for little return. I suggest that you be willing to consign to local stores, where you can keep an eye on things, but seldom to anyone you have to mail to. It's hard enough to collect from a local store on consignment, but trying to collect long-distance, *after* paying postage to send the zines, can be a losing venture.

By the way, whether you pay postage or bill the store for it is up to you, but generally, stores expect you to pay. Stores *should* pay postage on returns, however. You don't have to credit their returns if they are returned in unsellable condition, tagged, or otherwise too damaged – though you may get grief from stores when you try to enforce this policy.

In most stores, it may take three issues for a zine to catch on. Don't be disappointed if your first issue doesn't sell like hotcakes, or even your second. But if you're still not selling after the third try, then it's time to stop and think about it.

Stores are like people. Each has its own personality and way of doing things. Like people, stores are sometimes inconsistent. And, as with people, you will like some stores more than others. The good ones are supportive and professional (and probably read your zine!), while some are appalling in their utter lack of care or competence. You can always reduce shipments or refuse to continue stocking a store if they're giving you too much grief.

Distributors
If you don't want to mail your zines out one by one, you can contact a distributor who will sell your zine for you. There are two basic types of distributors ("distros" for short): small distros (often a single person) who deal in mail-order, and wholesale distros, who resell your zines to stores. There are certainly combinations of both, but most distros are clearly one or the other.

Mail order distros tend to be individuals who distribute zines because they're excited about them and may have an interest in a particular type of zine. Many do zines themselves, and distributing other zines they like is a logical extension of what they're already doing. In the punk and sci-fi scenes, for example, there are folks who sell zines at club shows, conventions, or other live events. Since these businesses tend to be small in scale and can come and go very quickly (like zines), finding good mail-order distros is a real accomplishment. But your cut of sales tends to be more negotiable (read: higher), and they tend to be easier to get money from than wholesale distros or stores. However, since most are so small, they tend to order about 5-10 copies of each issue.

Larger wholesale distributors, like AK Press and Last Gasp, often have websites and mail-order catalogs that will sell zines directly to individuals, but their bread and butter is selling to stores. They will take an agreed-upon number of copies at a heavy discount, usually 40/60 (meaning they pay you 40%), and resell these to stores, usually at 60/40 terms (meaning the store pays the distro 60%), so the distro makes about 20% on your zine for the time and trouble of distributing and collecting on it. Typically distros work on a consignment basis, so you have to wait for your money until some point after your next issue appears (usually 60 or 90 days in theory, but often longer in practice). Of course, wholesale distros get zines at a greatly reduced price compared to stores. The supposed advantage is that you make this up in volume.

There are advantages to dealing with a wholesale distro. They can get your zine into more stores than you would probably care to spend the time on yourself.

Unfortunately, there are plenty of stores, who will *only* deal with distros. You also lose some control over where your zine is sold. It is very improbable that your zine would ever be sold to chain stores or end up in places that are ethically objectionable. The only way this could happen was if people were special ordering it from a store frequently.

A little math makes the consignment distributor clearer. Let's say you're a modestly successful zine with a cover price of $3 and a print run of 3,000 copies. You send 50 copies of your zine at a 60% discount (meaning you get 40% for each copy sold). There are six returns at the end of the issue's cycle, which you then toss in the back issues pile for resale through your own direct mail catalog. They pay you upon receipt of your next issue, so you walk away with a check for 44 copies sold at $1.20 each, or $52.80, and you can still sell those six remaining copies. Not bad.

HINT: If a distributor is ordering more than they are selling, one tactic is to ship fewer copies, which may force the distro to send your zine only to the hottest-selling locations. Distros probably hate this idea, but from your perspective, it makes sense. Stores want their racks to look good, i.e., full, so they may order more zines than they can really sell, which would drive the sell-through percentages down. Magazine distributors are notorious for sending titles to places that didn't order them, because the distro believes that the store *should* order them. Often times the store buyer knows better than the distro and the zines get returned. Distributors will argue that having overstock adds to the visibility of your zine for *potential* sales and so unsold copies remain visible on shelves, which is bogus corporate speak. But who really suffers? Does the store lose sales because of this? No. Does the distributor lose money? No. Do you lose money? Almost all of it.

If you are particularly ambitious (or experimental) you could put an ISBN barcode on your zine and list it with Bowker – so it can be sold at places like Amazon.com, Baker & Taylor, Ingram, and special ordered by bookstores around the globe. Zines would technically quality as ISSN publications, but no one in the "industry" really knows what to do with them as such. An ISBN costs about $25 and you can purchase and register them with www.bowker.com

Distributor Alternatives:

An alternative to traditional distribution that fits very organically with zines is "do-it-yourself." While it is often not practical for a store to order copies of a single zine, if you work together with some friends to create your own distribution co-op of zines, it suddenly becomes practical for stores to order a cluster of zines together – especially if you synchronize releasing new issues. The various tasks, like soliciting orders or shipping copies, can be rotated between members of your group. This can greatly reduce the workload on each person and make it much more appealing for stores to deal direct.

ILLUSTRATION BY JULIA WERTZ • 2008 • WWW.FARTPARTY.ORG

Advertising and Publicity

Your best bet is to advertise in publications that are in the same area of interest as yours. A gardening zine, for instance, would probably not do well to advertise in a literary journal—unless you have done research and determined that a fair number of book readers are avid gardeners!

Most zines advertise by trading ads with other zines. **I highly recommend this.** Why? Because it's free, and it's mutual aid. Plus, every sale that ad generates is profit rather than simply offsetting the cost of an ad. Most zines could use more graphic images anyway, and ads help you to stay "connected" to other zinesters. This gives you someone to talk to when you have a question or problem.

There are several things you can do to increase the volume of responses to your ad:

Offer An Incentive. Give any sort of a deal, perhaps on a subscription or back issues. Maybe this is your chance to give away that stash of stickers you didn't know what to do with.

Use A Graphic In Your Ad. Make it as big and eye-catching as you can. If a picture can say a thousand words, use the picture and leave the words for when people contact you. A website can carry the bulk of your message. Mike Rodemann created a classic ad for his zine *9 1/2 Left* which simply featured a photo of a man holding a large fish pasted up with his address, the price, and the name of his zine. While it indicated nothing about his zine, it's an enticing picture that somehow works as an ad.

Use A Big, Bold Heading. Look through the pages of your favorite newspaper or magazine and notice which ads catch your attention. Chances are that they're the ones with the most interesting images, the boldest titles, and the most provocative phrases.

Be Inclusive. Your ad should target as many readers as possible. Make up several ads, and test them on friends, coworkers, loved ones, anyone who will give you useful feedback. Second opinions provide crucial objectivity and perspective. Other people will see things you missed, and they will miss things that you thought were obvious. Work on the more popular ads and polish them.

Another way to track responses in a certain publication or issue is to use a different email address in each one or code your ads by adding a fake department number to your address. If you have a post office box or a private postal mail box ("PMB"), you can use a dash followed by a two- or three-letter abbreviation right after your box number. Sometimes when you make a new issue it can be a good test to change your email address to see which issue people are responding to.

Mailing Lists
A zine generates a mailing list over its first few years, one way or another.

The best list, of course, is of people who have already purchased copies of your zine. Send them a flyer when you have a new issue ready. A postcard is even cheaper to send than a flyer, and the recipient doesn't have to open it. However, anything on it is visible to the casual observer – such as a postal employee – so be careful if your ad includes sensitive content or if your zine has a particularly controversial title. The zine *Midget Breakdancing Digest*, while not about what you might expect, had a hard time talking to printers.

You can also trade your list with other zines. It is considered courteous to get permission before you trade someone's name. You can include a check box on your order form or ad that allows people to add themselves to your open list.

Reviews

Reviews and word-of-mouth recommendations are probably the best promotion you can get for your zine, and best of all, they're free. If you aren't being reviewed in *Zine World*, *Xerography Debt*, and *Zine Thug*, you are missing a great opportunity to reach new readers. Jerianne and company review hundreds of zines in each issue of Zine World. All you have to do is fill out a questionnaire answering a few basic questions about your zine, and send a copy. You can use the form below, or print one out online at:
http://www.undergroundpress.org/submit-form.html .

PLEASE REVIEW THIS!
IT'S CALLED: _____
CREATOR'S NAME OR NOM DE PLUME: _____
ORDERING ADDRESS: _____
CITY: _____ STATE: ____ ZIP: _____
Email?: _____
Website?: _____
Include email/website in the review? ___Yes ___No
SINGLE COPY POSTPAID PRICE
(You'll get more orders if you clearly list a price)
to American addresses: _____
to Canadian addresses: _____
to Europe/Australia/World: _____
Is it available for trade? ___Yes ___No
Is it free to prisoners? ___Yes ___No
Available on audio cassette? ___Yes ___No
Statement of legal age required? ___Yes ___No
Anything else we should know?
_____
_____
_____
_____
_____

Single copies of Zine World:

A single copy of the current issue costs $4 to any address in the United States, $5 to Canada and Mexico, and $7 overseas: A Reader's Guide to the Underground Press PO Box 330156, Murfreesboro, TN 37133-0156 USA. You can also order a copy via PayPal for a bit extra, as well as a three-issue subscription. Accepts American cash (well-wrapped please, so the green can't be seen through the envelope), International Reply Coupons at $1 apiece, or unused American stamps. If you are sending more than a few dollars, please send a money order with "pay to the order of" made to Jerianne — not to Zine World. No checks. www.undergroundpress.org/order.html

Each issue features a section called "Publications," which is an excellent way to find others who will review your zine or who offer publications about publishing that you may find useful.

You can see some sample reviews at: www.undergroundpress.org/reviews.html .

Many other zines and magazines, especially the bigger punk ones like *Maximumrocknroll, Give Me Back, Razorcake,* and *Slug and Lettuce*, are another source of reviews (see the appendix in the back of this book). Similarly to stores, magazines that are thematically similar to your zine will often review it, even if they don't typically review zines. Zine reviews are a staple of most zines, and many other zine makers will trade copies of their publication for yours, just as they trade ads. This often leads to a review.

Zine readings and similar events can be very successful for keeping your zine's name in front of the local public. Put up flyers around town, send out press releases to calendar editors of local papers, and write about it on local messageboards. This way even people who don't attend the shows would have an idea about what you do.

Some zines make t-shirts, buttons, posters, stickers, patches, and all manner of paraphernalia emblazoned with their name. These are passive forms of promotion, and you don't often make your money back. Sure, you can sell t-shirts, but how many will you really sell and how many will you end up giving away? If money is tight and you can't find a cheap way to produce these, it might make more sense to save this money for something else.

On the other hand, *Clamor*, a magazine made by former zine editors, diversified its income, largely through the creation of an online "INFOshop", which allowed the name of their magazine to be cross-promoted through the purchase of related materials. It also created a steady stream of income with little effort. They employed friends to do the fulfillment and it became a self-running proposition.

Another option is CafePress.com, who print t-shirts and related items one at a time as people order them. While the prices are high (typically around $18 for a t-shirt) and you have significantly less control over how things look, many people stand by them because the work is taken care of for them.

Other simple things include: getting interviewed in another zine (some zines like *Maximum Rocknroll* are very open to interview submissions), on a community-access program, or on college radio; getting written up in the paper, making flyers or stickers for your zine and making a deal with other zines that you pass out each other's stuff with your mailorders; or approaching clubs for enthusiasts of your particular topic. This is particularly useful if your zine is a fan-oriented publication. There are also online fan groups covering everyone from Madonna to Noam Chomsky and your zine inevitably fits into some of these niche forums.

Magazines often send out sample copies to possible subscribers, but this is a costly proposition for you. You are probably best off just sending out review copies of your zine to everywhere that writes zine reviews. This creates much more visibility for your zine and is easy to track. Similarly, it can create some chatter if you send out free copies to higher circulation zine libraries and bedroom distros, who tend to talk to each other frequently and discuss new zines they've received and their favorites.

As with anything, use your imagination, and don't be afraid to ask others for help.

Fests, Conferences, Symposia
An "industry" event, like a zine convention or small press fair will create a great opportunity to sell or trade copies of your zine. If you have a lot of back issues you want to get rid of, this is an excellent way to do it. It is overwhelming to attend events like this, so people love to pick up free stuff to look at later. A personal connection with someone leaves them much more inclined to read your zine than a stranger that you pass a copy to. Check to see if any of the independent stores in your area are connected with these events.

There are literary fairs in most large cities, and it can be a great opportunity to travel and another place to distribute your zine or meet store buyers. In San

Francisco, for instance, the San Francisco Zine Fest takes place in the fall, the Alternative Press Expo in the summer, and the Anarchist Book Fair takes place at the end of March. Portland, OR hosts the Portland Zine Symposium which draws around 1,000 people every year in August and a half dozen smaller events distributed across the year. Ask your local bookstores about any such events. There are literally dozens of opportunities to sit behind a table with your zine every year in most cities. Sometimes you just have to be creative.

These events are great for getting your zine into the hands of stores, distros, libraries, and ultimately, readers. It's always preferable to hand someone a copy in person, as it begins a relationship which is much more real than business dealings through the mail. It also puts a face to your communication and tends to make people less likely to cheat you and more likely to understand where you are coming from. You should still follow up. If you review books, book fairs are also a great way to get on publishers' free book list.

More importantly, these events are also a great way to meet people, share your zine, and find new zines that can really challenge, impress, and encourage you. They are typically the most likely places to have life affirming moments about publishing and zines. These are the places where collaboration and friendships are born.

FLY • 05/2K8

copyright

Zine authors frequently ask about the need to copyright their work. They often fear theft from major corporations or their peers. Speaking purely along the lines of the law, these are not things to be concerned about. You have a lot of built-in protections just because your zine is published. Additionally, if or when your peers are stealing your work, copyright court is probably still not the best place to call them out about it.

A copyright protects an original artistic or literary work – like your zine. For copyright information, contact the Library of Congress at www.copyright.gov, (202) 707-3000, or write to: Copyright Office, Library of Congress, Washington DC 20559-6000. If you decide that copyrighting your zine is useful, you can download forms online at http://www.copyright.gov/forms/ or call the Forms Hotline at (202) 707-9100. There is a special copyright registration form for serials (a publication that is put out at regular intervals, like zines and magazines): Form SE. There is a different form for books, manuscripts, and speeches: Form TX. They can also provide a useful booklet, "Copyright Basics," which should answer many of your questions. This is also available online at http://www.copyright.gov/circs/circ1.html , or simply follow the home page at www.copyright.gov

Anyone can use a copyright symbol on their work to claim it as their own. All you have to do is include the phrase, "All contents Copyright © [year] by [your name]" with the appropriate date and name(s). By the way, if you don't have that cool copyright symbol, just type "(c)" instead.

Unless you have made special arrangements, you are copyrighting the *zine* as a literary work; normally, contributors to your zine retain the copyright to their individual work. If you send two copies of anything you publish to Register of Copyrights, Copyright Acquisitions Div., Library of Congress, Washington DC 20559-6000, this gives you a limited form of protection (Section 407). If you complete Form SE and send them $45, *per issue,* this provides a more complete form of protection (Section 408). However, if you don't want to let the Library of Congress know what you're up to (and we certainly wouldn't blame you for that), and you don't need the copyright protection, then why bother? And frankly, I'd be surprised to learn that anyone doing a zine was sending the LOC $45 per issue.

If you have a specific copyright violation concern (for instance, if you want to use or adapt someone else's work (especially outside the zine world), or you are concerned about others ripping off your work), I advise that you get the opinion of a lawyer. Paul T. Olson gives some advice on how to do this cheaply in the next section. However, you can also educate yourself about copyright law. To learn more, check out from your public library a copy of *The Writer's Lawyer,* by Roland L. Goldfarb and Gail E. Ross.

There are newer provisions for "Creative Commons" and Copyleft that are more in line with the ethics of most zines. Copyleft originated as a new way of looking at legal protections and rights for software around 1975. Programmers wanted their code to be used by other people, improved, modified, and shared – requiring that the same freedoms be applied to future modified versions. You can set the fine print of usage clauses and it has been since been expanded to music, art, and print documents.

Instead of allowing a work to fall completely into the public domain (with no copyright restrictions), copyleft allows the creator to impose some but not all copyright restrictions on those who want to engage in activities that would otherwise be considered copyright infringement. Under copyleft, usage infringement may be avoided if the would-be infringer continues the same copyleft arrangement.

Because of this, copyleft licenses are also known as viral or reciprocal licenses.

This is an appealing scenario for zinesters, as it frequently includes a non-commercial clause, meaning that anyone can reuse your work in their own non-profit zine or adapt things that you wrote to their own purposes. Often zinesters want to share their work but want to ensure certain protections that it won't be co-opted or used outside of their community and copyleft provides a good outlet for that.

There are six variations commonly employed for Creative Commons licensing:
1. Attribution (You must state who it was originally by)
2. Attribution + Noncommercial Use
3. Attribution + NoDerivs (You cannot change the original)
4. Attribution + ShareAlike (You can change and distribute a deriviative version)
5. Attribution + Noncommercial + NoDerivs
6. Attribution + Noncommercial + ShareAlike

According to the Copyright Office Basics brochure, "A work that was created (fixed in tangible form for the first time) on or after January 1, 1978, is automatically protected from the moment of its creation and is ordinarily given a term enduring for the author's life plus an additional 70 years after the author's death. In the case of 'a joint work prepared by two or more authors who did not work for hire,' the term lasts for 70 years after the last surviving author's death. For works made for hire, and for anonymous and pseudonymous works (unless the author's identity is revealed in Copyright Office records), the duration of copyright will be 95 years from publication or 120 years from creation, whichever is shorter."

As soon as a work is published, it is protected. You can prove that something is "published" by making a copy of it if it has a date printed on it. Sometimes people will mail a copy to themselves in order to have a post-marked date stamp. Leave the envelope sealed when it arrives.

Images
If I were trying to decide whether I could use an image, I wouldn't worry about anything over twenty-five years old. This is where protections end for printed materials. The thing to watch out for is if something has been re-published in that time period.

HINT: When in doubt, alter the image. This may still be considered "derivative," but should cover you if you change it enough. Three notable changes is considered standard. For instance, many artists use photos from magazines as references for their illustrations, but in the interpretation of a photo to a drawing, you could put the drawing right next to the photo and see little resemblance.

Trademarks

I'm presuming that no one reading this will want to register a trademark, but since there is some confusion about the difference between copyrights and trademarks, I am providing a bit of basic information.

According to the U.S. Department of Commerce, a trademark is a "word, phrase, symbol, or design, or combination of words, phrases, symbols, or designs, which identifies and distinguishes the source of the goods or services of one party from those of others." So a *copyright* protects an original artistic or literary work and a *patent* protects an invention.

You cannot copyright a title. To keep others from using it, you must register it as a trademark. National registration is very expensive, whereas California trademark is cheap, so register your trademark in California. If someone absolutely had to use your title, then this would force them to bypass 15% of the U.S. population, or otherwise rename their title for one state; not too convenient. In California, the office of the Secretary of State handles trademarks and service marks. Reach them at (916) 653-4984. Directory information for other state offices is at (916) 657-9900.

Zine publishers have occasionally gotten into trouble with large corporations for trademark infringement. In the 1990s, Mattel sent *Hey There, Barbie Girl* a cease-and-desist letter; the editor subsequently started a new zine without the word "Barbie" in it. From the same era, the publisher of *Bunnyhop* had to destroy all copies of an issue that had a Matt Groening parody on the cover. I wanted an illustrator to create a Miss Piggy look-alike to illustrate an article in my zine, but he told me that the Muppets were owned by Disney, who have a record for being litigious. So do eBay and Starbucks. Kieron Dwyer's *Lowest Common Denominator* showed an adapted Starbucks logo parody with the new text "Corporate Whore" and was promptly sued for trademark infringement.

Despite legitimate parody in these cases and many similar ones, the corporations usually win – through sheer volume of resources. Frequently, you can have powerful nonprofits on your side, but you are still battling batteries of lawyers and corporations that are hell bent on protecting their intellectual property.

So how do we get around this? Don't use the four consecutive letters e-b-a-y in your title or website and you will likely never hear from them. It should be okay to use an image that *evokes* the character you have in mind (an article about "Bugs Bunny" could use a generic rabbit, for example). If your project incorporates a trademarked product like Barbie, Miss Piggy, Bugs Bunny, or eBay, be very, very careful. The axiom "it's only illegal if they catch you" may apply here.

For an application or further information on trademarks, try: http://www.uspto.gov/ . You can also write: Assistant Commissioner for Trademarks, 2900 Crystal Dr., Arlington VA 22202-3513. For general trademark or patent information, call (703) 308-HELP; for automated, recorded general info, call (703) 557-INFO.

The Rad Possibilities of Creative Commons

By Katie Haegele

The other day I downloaded a philosophy class from MIT's website. All the course materials were free to me, even though I'm not a student—the readings list, the professor's notes, even the slide presentations. The reason I could do this is because MIT has published most of the content of almost all its classes as "OpenCourseWare" under a non-commercial, share alike, attribution copyright. This means, basically, that we can all look at and share the materials for free as long as we don't profit from them and give the proper attribution if we reproduce or quote from them. They don't even ask you to register. They're just giving it away.

As a writer, zinester, and reader, new ideas about creative ownership really excite me. It seems to me that these changes could mean all kinds of good things to us writers and artists, allowing us to disseminate our work further and share it more fully. Maybe it will ultimately help break the back of the ownership structure that the mainstream publishing world is built on, too. Wouldn't *that* be nice.

Ironically, I first started making zines because of a copyright question. A good few years ago I got really into making found poetry; everywhere I looked I saw a poem. Found poems are a kind of word collage, and to make one you use text that already exists—say, the owner's manual of an oven—and rearrange it in such a way that the words take on new meanings. What you're really doing is seeing the poetry that's already there and helping others to see it too. I'll give you an example. I made a poem from the Orienteering section of the 1948 edition of the <u>Boy Scout Handbook</u>, which I must have found at some rummage sale. "Find Your Way" was the name of the section, and that's what I called the poem. "With simple means/ and using your own personal measurements,/ determine a height you cannot reach/ and a width you cannot walk./ Call loudly for help if you are alone,/ and keep on calling." The book was talking about how to save yourself if you got lost in the woods, but it felt like a poem to me.

I wanted to share these poems with other people but I wasn't sure how. Wouldn't there be copyright problems if I tried to publish them? The Boy Scout book was old but some of my other sources were current, such as a list of movie titles from the Lifetime Television network. (Now **there** was a comic-poetry treasure trove.) For a while I didn't know what to do with my poems so I just carried them around in a notebook that I kept adding to obsessively. Then I remembered: zines! I'd always wanted to make a zine but hadn't known what I'd write about. These eccentric poems seemed like a good bet. I collected my favorite ones and asked an artist named Lesley Reppeteaux whose work I really like to make a drawing for the cover. I called the little collection *Word Math* and in all the years I've been making zines I've never stopped selling it.

Take the beautiful logic of found poetry a step further. What if people wrote things that they **wanted** other people to pass on or recycle in some way? Think of the ripple effect your work would have if you released it into the wild and it just kept going, getting turned into poems, appearing in other people's zines, being read into a microphone at a reading in some city you've never been to. My friend Roger Simian, an inventive soul from Scotland, wanted to include me in an issue of his zine *dumb/SULK trigg-er*. He decided the best way to tell people what my writing is like was to make a word salad out of it, stringing together sentences from poems, essays, and stories I'd written. They were my words but it was his story—his story of me. In this way his reading of someone else's writing became its own piece of writing. That's collaboration of a very powerful kind, a kind of consummation of the connection that's always made between writer and reader. I gave him permission to play with my writing like that, but what if I gave the whole world permission? It seems like the very idea of what it means to be an author could start to change. I get excited thinking about the new places we DIY publishers can go. Don't you?

what you must know about libel

by Paul T. Olson

Before we even start, you have to understand *legal advice comes from lawyers*; and I am not a lawyer. If someone is telling you they're gonna sue you for libel, you may want to get the opinion of a lawyer – even if you think the person threatening you is full of hot air. If you have any reason to believe that you could ever piss someone off with your zine, you should spend the time necessary to cultivate a friend or two in the legal profession. The peace of mind alone will be worth the trouble.

How do you do this? In the big world of mass media, the suits say, "Hey, I want you to be my lawyer. Here's a big bushel basket full of money." We're not gonna do this, are we?

HINT: The quickest and easiest way to get on the good side of the people whose good side you want to be on (and the bad side of people whose bad side you want to be on) is to join the American Civil Liberties Union. The Web makes it easy: http://aclu.org/ . Otherwise, you can call 1-888-567-ACLU. You can also check your phone book to see if your city has a branch office, or write to: ACLU,

125 Broad Street, 18th Floor New York, NY 10004. Amazingly, basic membership has not gone up in the last twelve years since this book was first published; it's still $20. As far as I can tell – at least, in Utah – there is also still a $5 a year limited income membership for students and other poor people. Please, though, send them at least $20 if you can. These are folks you want to support. You could mention in your zine that you're a member of the ACLU – a plug for them sure wouldn't hurt, either. If you have an office of the ACLU in your town, make sure they are on your mailing list.

Contact your local Legal Aid Society or your city's equivalent. Every town is different; they all offer different services and have different intake criteria.

Make friends with law school students. Leave some copies of your zine at the local law school. Law school students love to talk about the stuff they're studying. Plus, law school students have this weird habit of turning into lawyers.

If all else fails, put a small ad in your zine (the smaller the better – lawyers love small print), saying: "Hey! Lawyers reading this zine? I have a question," or something similar. Leave it lying about the law school and mail it to your nearest ACLU office and Legal Aid Society.

Libel, Slander, and Defamation
Libel is defamation in print. Yes, even your small zine counts as print. In 1983, the Altoona Telegraph sent a memo to a U.S. Justice Department investigator asking for confirmation of suspicions they had that Mafia money was going to a local building company. The memo went to federal bank regulators, and the bank canceled the builder's line of credit. The builder sued. The jury found the allegations in the memo to be false, and the paper was shit-out-of-luck even though they had never actually published a story about it. Their copied and circulated memo constituted publication.

Slander is spoken defamation. For our purposes, we won't be discussing slander.

Defamation is language (spoken or written) that adversely affects someone's reputation.

Who can be libeled?

Any living person or business. Dead people cannot be libeled. Yeah! Elvis is fair game! Unless he's not really dead.

How can a plaintiff prove that you've committed libel?

To prove that you have committed libel, the plaintiff (person who said that you've libeled him or her by something you've said in your zine) must prove all four of the following:

1)You used defamatory language.
2)The language actually referred to the plaintiff. This is important to note – not referring to someone by name is not necessarily going to keep your ass out of trouble.
3)The defamatory language was published.
4)The defamatory language damaged the plaintiff's reputation.

You'll have to prove one of the following:

"The language I used was not defamatory!" Yeah, right.

"I wasn't referring to the plaintiff!" I would not trust this defense. Mainly because you'll most likely have to say who you were referring to (and possibly face a libel suit from them); but also, you're leaving yourself in the hands of the jury. Juries are different from angry mobs in two ways: (1) Juries are generally better dressed than angry mobs; and (2) You can reason with an angry mob.

"It wasn't published!" This defense will cause the plaintiff's lawyers to pee their pants laughing as they slap themselves with copies of your zine.

"It didn't harm the plaintiff's reputation because I was just expressing my *opinion!* Hmm. Maybe you're *not* doomed.

The guide here is: "Is it possible to prove the statement wrong?" If so, you are in trouble. Let's say that your zine runs restaurant reviews. Let's say that you write, "The Rusty Sabre's food has been giving people salmonella." If you can't prove they have – you may be doomed.

Pure opinion is protected speech. You write, "The Rusty Sabre serves bad food." "Bad" is a matter of opinion; the Rusty Sabre could say, *"Belgian Money Hump Zine* is bad." So what? You can't prove it either way – it's a value judgment.

Name-calling is considered to be almost-but-not-quite pure opinion. You could write: "The owner's an asshole!" "Asshole" is a nasty name but not *provably* true or false. If you said he was "insane," or "alcoholic" (and he wasn't), you would be doomed, because those are diseases diagnosable by a doctor. Hell, even if he was, you might be vulnerable to an invasion of privacy lawsuit, which is a totally different thing, but every bit as dangerous as a libel suit.

Ridiculous hyperbole is considered pure opinion. You could say: "Dogs for miles around began howling with fear when the waitron brought out my entrée." Well, obviously this did not happen – it's hyperbole! The less obvious the hyperbole, the less safe it is.

A lot of times you can mix fact with opinion: "The Rusty Sabre's chef never went to cooking school and that's why the food sucks." This mixes a provable fact and an opinion – contingent on whether or not the chef actually went to cooking school. Common sense dictates that this would be a weird thing to say in a review, unless your zine specializes in nonsequiturs, which is entirely likely.

If you cannot keep them from proving all four items, you might still escape by using the defense, "Yes, I wrote defamatory language about the plaintiff with reckless disregard for the truth, but the plaintiff is a public official or public figure and therefore has to tolerate this scrutiny!"

Public officials are not able to clobber you for libel because the courts have decided it is important to the functioning of democracy for individuals, no matter how small, to examine, lampoon, and even pillory the poor bastards. This is why you can say that George W. Bush is a cocaine-snorting, womanizing, draft-dodger, even if you cannot prove that he did any of these things. So who's a public official? The President, congressmembers, governors, and mayors – definitely. Who else? Teachers, court reporters, crossing guards? In some states they are – but not in others. Well, you gotta ask yourself this question: "Do I feel lucky?"

Public figures are less safe targets, but are generally described as people who voluntarily embroil themselves in public controversy. Some examples would be Michael Moore, Jane Fonda, William F. Buckley Jr., L. Ron Hubbard, and Louis Farrakhan. This is less clear than who is or is not a public official, and it puts you in more danger. Note that O.J. Simpson is not on this list of public figures. Why not? Because people accused of a crime do not automatically become public figures. Remember: The accused is *assumed* to be innocent until proven guilty. Even when defendants are found guilty, they can keep to themselves and avoid the label of "public figure."

A public figure for limited purposes is the least safe target. These are people who may be public figures within a certain sphere or for a short period of time. R. Seth Friedman *might* be considered a public figure within the zine world, but not the larger world. Dennis Kucinich *might* be considered a public figure for purposes of the 2008 Democratic primaries, but not all the time. The president of the Concerned Citizens' Committee for Citizens' Concerns *might* be a public figure in your hometown, but not on a national level.

Sticking to items that you can prove are the truth is not a defense against invasion of privacy – which is another thing altogether. For information on invasion of privacy (which is the *other* big thing zinesters need to worry about) or more information about libel, check your local public library. In addition to weighty, unreadable tomes about law, they'll have well-written, easily skimmable books. Use the table of contents and index to look up just the stuff you need, and ignore the rest.

What else can you do to protect yourself? You are probably already doing it. Your best defense against libel is to stick to expressing your opinions – and really, folks, isn't the desire to express your opinion the reason you started your zine in the first place?

computers

The best computer for making zines is the one you can get to most easily. Folks who do graphic design tend to prefer Macs, but this probably means little in the limited capacity that zines tend to rely on computers (if any).

The important thing is to have *access* to a computer, if you want one. You don't necessarily need to own a computer in order to have access to one, any more than you need to own a copier in order to make copies. Why invest a small fortune in purchasing lots of gear when you can use a friend's, use one at work, or have an excuse to go to your local library? A desktop publishing system will probably cost you about $0-500, depending how savvy you are at acquiring things. A simple computer, a laser printer, and a flatbed scanner are all you would really need. There is an open source piece of free software called Scribus that has all of the functionality of expensive commercial desktop publishing programs like Quark Xpress or Indesign – except it's free!

One option is to buy a used computer via a reputable store that offers a warranty. You can also try the want ads, or online equivalents such as craigslist or eBay, but this is risky; you could end up with a lemon and no way to get your money back. It pays to do some research so you get what you really need. Get the biggest monitor you can afford. If you've got the desktop space for it, older-style CRT monitors are going for a song, which might make it worth the risk – just make sure you don't have to pay a small fortune for shipping. Get as much RAM and hard disk space as you can afford; you always end up wanting more memory and storage, so start out with the most you can get for the money. Since computers seem to become "obsolete" every two years or so, someone is always getting rid of one that would be a perfect home publishing computer.

If you're buying hardware or software, the best deals are often at the big online / mail-order catalogs like Tiger Direct. Ordering from an out-of-state vendor avoids paying sales tax. If you don't know computers, you may be better off buying from a local establishment that can offer more hand-holding and a convenient place to go for repairs and upgrades.

Some people think they need to learn a fancy layout program in order to publish a zine. It is completely unnecessary unless that is the look that you really want. An X-acto knife, hand waxer, and a typewriter can produce a fabulous zine. Paul Olson once said, "Garbage in, garbage out. If you have no eye for layout or editorial sense, *no* program can help you. If you're sharp, glue and scissors are fine."

What about a printer? Which one should I buy? An inkjet will do for a low-budget zine, though laser printers are smear-proof and produce sharper masters. Sometimes you can get a great deal on a used laser printer, but be sure it has a money-back guarantee. Laser printers last forever so buying used is safer than with most printers.

If you use a laser printer, set it to 1200 DPI (dots per inch) resolution, and apply any other sharpening controls your printer software may have, before you print your masters. The higher the resolution, the sharper your graphics and type will look.

An inkjet will give you the option of color output, but it is unlikely that you will be able to produce a color zine. It's probably a wasted feature unless you are printing very few copies and use your inkjet as the "press." This quickly gets expensive too.

HINTS: Use the best paper available for your masters – your copies will look sharper. It pays to splurge a bit in this department. For laser printers, some coated stocks work quite nicely. You can also buy special smooth-finish laser paper. If you get an inkjet, buy the special inkjet paper to get the crispest image. It can be expensive, but you don't have to use it for your drafts, just the final output. For drafts, you can use regular copier paper.

In a similar vein, the cartridge you use to print your final draft should be the newest one you have. I recommend buying a cartridge dedicated solely to printing out your masters. When it's been used a bit (i.e., when blacks are no longer their absolute blackest), convert it to general-purpose use and buy another.

John P. '08

compiling back issues

Sometimes the idea of making especially thick issues of a zine seems like a great idea until you are stuck endlessly removing jams from the copy machine and having to carry home the equivalent of ten reams of paper. The idea of approaching an offset printer comes up now and again as a sometimes affordable option for printing an especially large issue or anthologizing back issues of a zine.

A printer will generally have a checklist to go through before you go to print. This ensures the lowest chance of error. Be sure to ask a lot of questions and get at least 3 quotes from different printers before you commit to a particular one. If you are unsure about something, ask before you stand to make a critical error. Ask your friends who have worked with a printer before. They may be able to explain things in layperson's terms.

After you send your book to the printer they'll convert everything to printing plates and make a sample copy before they print all of your books. This is called a proof. You have the option at this point to change any graphical placement, spelling, or grammar errors before you are stuck with an entire print run of your book. You are most likely going to put at least a few thousand dollars into this project. Make sure that you will end up with something you will be happy with.

A big part of your book is, of course—the cover. Books are judged by the cover no matter how many proverbs will tell you to do the opposite. Do you have artistic or design skills to make it visually appealing? If not, do you have a friend who does?

If you are creating your book on the computer, virtually no printer will accept MS-Word files and will want the final product setup as a PDF, Indesign document, or Quark file. If you are using Scribus, you will most likely have to submit an exported PDF file. These are simple programs to learn and use but it will most likely be to your benefit to do so before crunch time when the book should be leaving for the printer.

Be very leary of any printer that does accept MS-Word files, as they are likely a print-on-demand printer that will assign large fees to layout and typeset your work for you. It is not uncommon for places like this to charge an extra thousand dollars to make your work "ready for print", which most people with a library card could eventually do themselves.

A common problem is page margins. Check with your printer before laying out your pages; especially if you are doing more extensive artistic layouts. If you want the artwork to extend off the page this is called a "bleed". You'll need to extend the artwork past the cut marks on the page between 1/8" and 1/2" (depending on the printer's specifications) . If you don't want a bleed you'll want to make sure to keep everything at least 3/8" or more away from the edge. This helps the final product trim down and look better in the end as well as making it easier for the printer.

After you have a basement full of books the next logical step is to put those books in the hands of people who want them. The most efficient way to do this is through book distributors. One of the primary advantages of working with distributors is they will likely have more luck getting your books into stores than you will on your own. Stores are more suited to buying a few copies of many different books from a distributor than buying many of the same title from a publisher.

Depending on the subject matter of your book it may open or close doors with distributors. For example, AK Press (www.akpress.org) deals largely with independently published hard-left leaning books and pamphlets. Last Gasp (www.lastgasp.com) specializes in small press comics and books of all sorts, with a healthy focus on drugs and erotica. Stickfigure (www.stickfiguredistro.com) is a punk distributor who is relatively friendly to small print-run books and zines. Marginal (www.marginalbook.com) is a Canadian distributor who seems quite friendly to small publishers. Small Press Distribution (www.spdbooks.org) is a non-profit book distributor.

A problem that you may run into is that other book distributors (Perseus, Consortium, SCB, National Book Network, etc) are exclusives – meaning that you can work only through them and that other distributors and stores can only buy your books through them.

shawn granton ★ may 2008

touring: when in reno, eat the raw pie!

I've organized and gone on about six different zine tours, with the more recent ones incorporating video as well. After some setup and planning we found out that others had done similar things in the past and I set out to learn more about how they had gone about it.

Initially we had a lot of questions: What would we do? Who would come to the shows? Where would we perform? And another big question was *why?*

We decided to tour because we all felt that it would be a good way to meet people and promote our zines to people that didn't know about them—or zines in general! While this may seem like a staggering task, it was really quite easy.

I combed all of my old resources for booking tours (for bands) and bookstore contacts that sold our zines. Between these and talking to a few friends who had either visited the remaining cities or had a friend there, we had a pretty complete list of venues to perform in. We ended up performing in people's houses, coffee shops, art galleries, punk venues, infoshops, rock clubs, bookstores, and libraries. Really, the options are

even broader than that but these were the venues that fell into place for us.
I began endlessly making phone calls day and night. It seemed eternal for awhile.
Either the events coordinator was not in when I called or they were busy or away.
The list was getting longer instead of shorter. I was also a stranger. This process
became vastly easier on subsequent tours because I had some contact with the
people involved.

Slowly but surely venues started to confirm dates and we had a pretty complete tour
set up. In general, if I could speak to the person in charge of events and had a concise
explanation of what we were going to do – read zines and play videos, they either said
yes or no. A few of the bookstores asked for samples of our zines before agreeing
completely but once they received them they all wholeheartedly agreed to do it. One
problem that we ran into was that sometimes when we sent our zines to booking
places, someone else intercepted the package, got excited about the zines, and took
them home themselves, instead of leaving them for the promoter. Fortunately, this
was normally seen as a testament to their quality and got us booked.

An alternative to calling venues is to e-mail them. I didn't have much luck with
this method in my life as it is quite easy to ignore e-mail. Most of the time venues
and bookstores are buried in e-mails anyway and it is easier to get an answer over
the telephone.

I set up the first tour, consisting of about 28 shows in 26 days, in a little under
two months. We were releasing a book by the *Urban Hermitt* and the tour
coincided with the book's release. Our schedule was pretty tight but everything
sort of worked out for the best. We didn't have any shows fall through and we
only decided to cancel one from the road (It was a coffee shop full of cops and
homophobic posters).

After you have dates setup at venues the next step is promoting your shows. We
sent out postcards to people who ordered our zines in all of the states we were
visiting and sent out e-mails to all of our friends. After that we had our friends in
those cities put up flyers in case the venues didn't sufficiently promote the shows.
Something I have mixed feelings and results with is sending out press releases to
weekly and daily newspapers about events. It is really successful at getting little
mentions of your event in the papers and is good for drawing people that aren't
necessarily interested in zines or part of a young, progressive community that
would be out noticing flyers. However, the trade off is that few articles represent
the event remotely accurately, and in my opinion and there is a certain amount of

discomfort dealing with the press, as they are often writing a nonexistent angle into the story.

We didn't need to get vendors licenses to sell things on tour as the places we went to were (mostly) commercially legal bookstores or venues. To some people it might be appealing to take a more guerilla approach to touring (like performing on the street or selling out of the trunk of your car) but that could also complicate some of the legal matters. I've met people who've had tremendous success with this method though.

A major problem that we had on tours was lack of space in our touring vehicle. None of us owned cars ourselves so scrounging together a touring vehicle was complicated. On the first two tours we had 5 people and the resulting amount of zines, books, and personal possessions. Loading up a vehicle with all of our things we barely had room to breathe at times and personal comfort was thrown out the window. Also on a tight budget, we used small vehicles to conserve gas and environmental impact, which was more important than material comforts most of the time.

Starting on the third tour we got a month-long car rental which was about $600 (though now seems to cost closer to $900). This seemed like a bargain for a month long tour but the thing that we didn't count on is that we spent another $1,000 on gas! We did a few university shows which covered the bulk of the bills.

Money was never a huge problem because we slept on floors, ate at grocery stores and diners (out of our own pockets or from selling zines at shows), and paid for our gas from the donations accumulated at shows. Car repairs were the only substantial expense and were covered by selling things and collecting donations.

I think touring with your zine should occur more often in the zine community. It's a great way to promote something and a great way to turn a road trip into an organized, focused affair and make new friends. Also, when you tour with your zine, it makes it that much more acceptable for other people to do it. If you have any questions, comments, tips, advice, or need/want to share a contact in a specific town just drop a line—joe@microcosmpublishing.com

always bring a pillow!

participation

Zines are a subculture that is active and participatory, with little separation between performer and audience. It is very common for people who spend a few years making zines to become entrenched in the community in other ways. Zine publishers become distro operators, internet forum hosts, zine librarians, and organizers of zine conferences, as a natural extension of their love for zines.

It is in this way that the community can grow and change over time, with resources that enable you to talk to your peers on a level playing field. It is also these resources that sustain the energy flow and finances of the zine world. For example, when Jenn Wilson, organizer of the San Francisco Zine Fest and Starfiend Distro, moved to Vancouver—John Porcellino, author of *King Cat,* picked up the reins of organizing the fest—until he too moved back to Illinois—when it was taken over by Calvin Liu.

There are many other simple examples. Korinna Irwin of *Rockstar with Words* zine founded Youth in Revolt Distro in Arcata, CA. After three years and a move to Portland, she handed the reins of the distro to her friend Megan back in Arcata. Similarly Arcade Distro, Basement Children, and Stranger Danger Distro have all changed hands.

But not all projects are just passed around endlessly, either. Most distros and fests start from scratch as old ones fade away in distant cities and towns. Ciara Xyerra started Learning to Leave a Paper Trail distro after half a dozen other places closed up shop, including the long-running Pander Zine Distro. Even though she was geographically quite distant from many of the former distros, she was still occupying the same niche.

Similarly, recently new zine fests have popped up in Austin, TX, Minneapolis, MN, London, England, and Richmond, VA. Even long-running and extremely well attended zine events like the Portland Zine Symposium, Expozine in Montreal, and Canzine in Toronto have been running for less than ten years.

The Portland Zine Symposium is organized by a rotating cast of about a dozen people, who are involved to varying degrees, and seems to have a totally new set of organizers every few years. This change is healthy, as it demonstrates a critical mass present in the subculture. As some people burn out or find themselves unable to participate as frequently, others take their place. And it's not always a matter of trading places, either – many new distros, fests, and libraries appear out of thin air – driven by their sheer passion for their craft.

The Toronto Zine Library grew very quickly into a very focused organization, with a vast collection built from scratch. Older libraries are passed on, or donated to other collections like the old Epicenter Library in San Francisco, currently housed in Smurph's closet but looking for a public home. When *Factsheet 5* closed its metaphorical doors, its vast collection of zines, perhaps the largest in existence, was donated to the NY State Library in Albany.

Other places like the Zine Archive and Publishing Project in Seattle and The Independent Publishing Resource Center (IPRC) in Portland, OR operate within the legit realm with some paid staff, legal status, and public buildings with open hours. Even though these entities are organized as legitimate non-profits, their staff still has the ability to regularly rotate and shift as people move on and excited newcomers move to town.

This is all just the tip of the iceberg. The ways that you can participate in the larger zine subculture are entirely based on what you can dream up. Alan Lastufka, Kate Sandler, and Aaron Cynic of the *Fall of Autumn* created a series of downloadable free-use clip art that people can use in their zine from popular zine artists as well as a long-running series of downloadable podcasts of zinesters reading from their zines and being interviewed.

The Anchor Archive in Halifax, NS is a zine library and distro that hosts brunches, has public hours, and a hosts a resident zine-maker who lives in the adjacent shed for a month while they focus on producing new zine work.

Grrrl Zines A Go Go in San Diego is a community program that conducts public events and workshops featuring zines as a form of outreach. Like the IPRC, they collaborate with schools and other organizations to add zines to their programming.

A really simple thing that you can do is host zine-making parties with your friends, where you come together to be creative, clack away on typewriters, and share in the joy of the creative process!

Some distros, like Tree of Knowledge and Basement Children, existed for over a decade without a proper website by tabling at events of all stripes, including punk shows, zine fests, and local gatherings. Before opening an infoshop in Dublin, Ireland, Natalia and Willie had a weekly Sunday brunch at their house in New Orleans, where people could browse zines and books that they had for sale.

Since most distros, libraries, and resources do not actively compete with each other, and tend to interact as friends in a community, helping each other out, people who are currently active in the zine community are a great place to start when you are developing your ideas.

Understanding the responsibility and time commitment of undertaking projects for no pay is an important thing to think about. Many distros and libraries never see the light of day or fizzle out as soon as the summer ends.

You can prevent these problems by honestly evaluating how much time you have to commit to the project by answering the following questions.

1) What kind of project do you want to operate?
2) What is your ultimate goal with the project? Write it out in one sentence as your mission statement.
3) What kind of legal structure do you want to have, if any? Will there ever be efforts to provide wages or stipends?
4) What kind of time commitment do you have to commit to the project?
5) Will other people help you? Will you be able to relinquish control for the benefit of collaborating and sharing the work with others?

6) If you work with other people, what kind of operating structure will you have?
7) How will you fundraise?
8) Where will the money come from to start the project? How much are you willing to sink in?
9) Why do you want to do this? Be honest with yourself.
10) How will your organization be sufficiently different from other, similar organizations?
11) How will you spread the word about your project?
12) Will you continue to be interested in working on it if it isn't getting as much attention as you had initially hoped?
13) Do you honestly have the time and money to commit to it?

Remember, it's supposed to be about having fun and contributing positively. Be nice to people and be conscious of when it is generating stress. You will often end up in a position where you are teaching new or curious people the ropes, which can require extra patience. Go hang out at zine conferences, as it's one of the best ways to get a great feeling that you are contributing and involved with something culturally important.

the anchor archive, Halifax, NS

ethics

In conducting the interviews to research this chapter, I continually stumbled upon something that seemed strange. Most of the issues that people talked about were theoretical probems that people feared but were not issues people were presently experiencing.

But there are plenty of issues that people are experiencing. Becca Confidential of *Darling Disasters* is worried about people using "someone else's stuff without asking them first." Claudia McBarron of the zine *Subgroup Cursive* wants to find "a broader appeal that goes beyond the initial science fiction and punk roots" and have "communication be a person to person event rather than through a corporation."

"I think the overall values of zine makers are inherently the same... free speech, corporate-free literacy, personal power. I think it is important to find common ground." Similary, Becca thinks ethics are important to discuss because "You really don't want to piss people off who are in the independent media area. They'll bite your head off worse than any kind of judge or anyone. I love this community."

Craven Rock has different feelings on the matter. "The rise of the 'zinester' and the D.I.Y kids' co-optation of the culture is at the cost of the writer/artist who just uses an available medium. If somebody said "the book community" [it would] be ludicrous, as this ends up dictating content and is offensive. The idea of a "zine community" instead of something more specific like "the bike zine community" or "the polyamory zine community is dictating ethics.

I feel like I'm put into the whole new school zinester box when someone finds out I do a zine. I feel limited by the context. I am a writer who happens to be perfectly happy doing a zine, besides that dilemma, anyway.

Since computer blogging has become the dominant empowering and accessible medium for the independant writer, zines became popular with people who fetishized the medium itself for its archaic and quaint qualities. Since zines were becoming less popular, [newcomers] basically had a scorched earth policy to claim zines as their own. No longer was it the 'voice crying in the wilderness,' instead it turned into an unalienated scene. This scene also liked certain things (vegan cooking, bikes, making out, polyamoury) and as long as you wrote subject matter within their field of interest you could be a part of this scene. People who didn't care for this subject matter are now alienated. It is unethical to make an entire medium a "safe place" where your particular subculture won't be offended or hurt. When zines first started there was room for everybody from Bob Black to Jim Goad. I don't care for Jim Goad myself, but I am also an adult and can decide on my own whether or not I want to read him."

Claudia teaches kids of ages 6-17 the skills of zine-making in order to create zines made by youth for youth. She also feels limited by their existing scope. "I think it is important to have all age zines out there. The younger students literally walk around hugging their freshly published zines. Not every parent wants to have their child reading about someone's uterus. Not every child wants to be reading about someone's uterus."

With no editor or boss over your shoulder you are free to do as you please. Douglas Waltz does the entertainment zine *Divine Exploitation*. In a recent issue he interviewed a woman who "sent [photos] and then the next day said that I could only use one of them. It was one that I had not planned on using. I thought it was a little odd, but I honored her wishes. I also killed the article. Now, I had these pics and could have run with them anyway, but I really think it best to honor your interviewees."

Additionally, issues of free speech were important to those interviewed, and not just protecting their own freedom of speech. Claudia says "[It's important to] listen to individuals that hold values that might not be your own in the name of free speech."

Responsibility

Different folks have different values. Some people believe that it is unethical to sell zines on eBay. Others want to have a very firm control over exactly how and where their zine is handled, and thus are wary of working with distributors who would work as a middle man and sell their zine to stores and readers that are disconnected from them. In that sense a zine becomes more and more like a product than an exchange of ideas or a community. Some people refuse to deal with specific distributors or stores—or stores or distributors at all! Some people believe strongly in copyleft and believe that all zines should be able to be copied freely by anyone. Many people reprint articles from zines without asking the author.

Entire distros exist that thrive on selling zines that they've copied without permission and reproduce third and fourth generation copies of varying quality. Sometimes this is justified under the idea of "creative commons". They aren't making money from it other than what is being re-invested into the distro, so by their understanding of the way zines operate, it is okay. Understandably, some zinesters are very upset about this and go to great lengths to try and prevent their zines from being copied without their permission.

A zine can be a great place to explore and express your feelings, and to say things you have always wanted to say, but once something is printed and distributed, there is no way to recall it, and there is always the chance that every single person you know could see what you have printed. You should believe and be able to stand up for what you print. The one who creates the publication is ultimately responsible for everything printed.

Zines, post-riot grrrl and in the arge of the internet, have become somewhat more of a sounding board for people's thoughts and feelings. Oftentimes, it feels like people do not evaluate the results of their words on others. Zines can hurt feelings and wreck relationships. Your partner or friend will not always appreciate the artistic creative non-fiction literary device that you spun around their lifestyle. When you interpret your friends, even as fictionalized characters in a story, it is normally still obvious to them and can hurt their feelings.

Similarly, "calling someone out" in your zine can be very damaging to their life. Be aware and certain that you are ready to be part of an emotionally taxing and difficult discourse. There are various zines created around personal conflicts, relationships, or feuds that zinesters have been involved in. The zine *Kool Man* is used to expose Robert Dupree's deceitful and scandalous habits, including fake characters that he creates to encourage women to have sex with him. Countless zines are used to discuss and purge descriptive acts of sexual abuse and rape. Sometimes the authors do this for the purpose of outing other zinesters as abusive, sometimes as way just to put traumatic events in perspective, and sometimes no names are mentioned at all.

Pen Names are common, but should not be used as a way to avoid the personal responsibility of what you write. If you are looking to accept checks, this can also get tricky. You will also have to make your own policy on who you will and won't accept money from. Some people are comfortable taking money from prisoners. Some won't deal with them at all. Some give them zines for free because their hourly wage is piddly.

Ingenuity
When I first started doing a zine in high school, the most frequent question from my peers was "How did you know that you could do that?" to which there is no answer other than, "I saw people that I could relate to, who were doing it themselves." Similarly, zines can open up this entrepreneurial spirit to the whole world if you let them.

The sheer volume of zine creation and people's need to express themselves has led zine makers to dozens of different techniques for stealing photocopies in large volume, learning to clean postmarks off of stamps and reuse them, applying aspects of creative reuse (using an item that can be acquired cheaply for something other than its intended purpose), using library reference materials and microfilm, learning and developing artistic skills, and digging through the trash to find office supplies. We have learned economies of barter and found value in things beyond simple dollars and cents. Zines teach more than these literal methods. They promote thinking about the sheer possibilities of a self-directed life.

I sincerely believe that these things have been very healthy for the personal development of myself, my peers, and the vast majority of people who make zines – not as a way to manufacture career criminals, but as a way to learn self-expression and alternatives to spending money. In a political sense, this is a refreshing development for a consumer culture. Zine makers are learning ingenuity and innovation through their peers, methods and techniques that extend to all aspects of our lives.

Through these methods, and deconstruction of corporate culture and norms, zine makers have learned to live within the margins and build our own community with these ideas—creating collective housing, learning the medicinal properties of plants, creating community centers, making films—without a budget, and pushing the envelope of what is possible through these mediums.

Perhaps most importantly though, zines encourage us to push the bar higher.

Why can't I start my own bookstore or a bicycle shop? With the same applied hard work, ingenuity, and community effort, we can build institutions that are developed from our ideas birthed in zines.

Mr. Mike, a former Kinko's employee from Minneapolis, took his passion for and skills learned from zines and applied it to homesteading. He founded his own new town of four people and was elected as mayor.

Growth and Change
The herd of zine publishers has thinned, partially due to the attention subsiding from zines around 1999, and partially the fact that some people were drawn to zines as a way of putting their diary into words, and can find avenues to do that just as well through blogging. The zines that remain, and those that pick up the torch, are producing at a much higher standard. Ideas are much more developed and elaborated on. Zine aesthetics are at an all time high. People put a lot more time and effort into hand printing beautiful, multi-colored covers. Political ideas are bringing new thoughts and ideas to the discussion. Skillshare zines are putting a lot of time into creating clear instructions. People who continue to publish zines in the 21st century follow that pursuit because it appeals to them on a personal and individual level.

Oftentimes people have complicated circumstances. They've pursued a non-paying craft for 15 years and are now 30 and can't afford to spend hours each week working on their zine for free. Maybe they are disabled or need a steady source of income. Sometimes people take the skills they've learned and use those to pursue a job or attempt selling their craft to people who have money.

Carol Parks draws a five figure salary by marketing her zines and zine-making workshops to middle aged housewives. She charges prices that would probably not be acceptable to most of the zine community and in return provides empowerment and a hobby to these women—a hobby that offers self-expression and doesn't demand a rigorous skill set.

Often people move to projects other than zines for the simple reason that artistically they feel they've learned and conveyed all that is possible for them. More than anything else, this is the single most expressed reason that zine writers decide to publish books or move to other kinds of journalism. Even in the best-case scenarios, these jumps are not financially motivated, as the money is just not there.

Every so often there is a rumbling in the zine community about how so-and-so has just signed a contract with a book publisher, or sold their zine through a mainstream magazine distributor, or made their zine to appeal to the "mainstream market". Sometimes, even when you are fully independent, just the sheer perception that you are "too large" is cause for demonization. This implies to some a betrayal of DIY ethics. There is a near-constant debate about whether zines like *Maximum Rock n Roll* are still zines.

Sometimes zines make the leap into magazine territory. This is neither stigmatized nor celebrated, necessarily. *Bust* and *Giant Robot*, two popular magazines available at most newsstands, both started out as stapled and folded photocopies with low print runs. Now they're glossy magazines with ads and a barcode, available virtually anywhere you look.

Some feel a magazine being scanned by a beeping electronic wand in a big box bookstore, purchased by someone casually interested in the featured artist on the cover, doesn't have the same personal connection between writer and reader as a zine being mailed directly from the editor with a nice letter. Rebecca Gilbert defines a zine in the documentary *$100 & A T-Shirt* as "being motivated by something other than money." This is a commonly held belief in the community.

In-fighting

Perhaps it's simply humans' propensity to gossip about other people's lives and projects, but zinesters love to gab about and critique each other behind their backs. What's hotter than a rumor that a storied zinester is pregnant or that someone broke the unspoken code of ethics.

Some people heavily involved with zines are frustrated with their opposition to vast power structures—like the US government's ongoing war in the Middle East. Fighting power and battles on this scale can feel like butting your head up against a wall. Perhaps, for some, people in your community are more accessible and it can be easy to take out your frustrations on someone that your actions can have an affect on.

The *Williamette Week* in Portland, OR did a story studying whether or not Starbucks Coffee was hurting local businesses. The most surprising finding was that contrary to popular belief, a Starbucks in a neighborhood generally increases coffeshop traffic at all cafes—independent and corporate. The assumptive reasoning is that more people start drinking coffee. Similarly, zines in a more visible place expose more people to zines. So when more local zine action appears, people have already been exposed to zines, and are more receptive. Moe Bowstern of *Xtra Tuf* zine explains that "a rising tide lifts all boats."

Conclusion

Zine publishers, first and foremost, are motivated by love of their work. They would not be reaching this plateau if they had not been putting in free labor for all these years. That said, it can be hard to understand the difficult decisions, problems, and motivations of someone who is working on a larger scale. The vast majority of zinesters begin in their teens. Some start even younger. Some start in college. Very few start in their 30s or older. A person's needs, abilities, problems, responsibilities, and motivations change—especially over the course of ten or fifteen years of publishing.

There are zine editors who want to have their cake and eat it too—achieve a level of commercial success while attempting to remain true to their underground roots—or eschewing the mainstream success to which they aspire. While I don't like hypocrisy, I don't fear it, either. We don't exist in a binary world and things are simply more complicated than that. I have witnessed financial hardships that forced decisions that editors or publishers would not have made otherwise.

I do think that if "making it" preoccupies your mind, then it likely drives your writing and affects its quality negatively. Opportunists are everywhere, and like any other underground culture, the zine world certainly attracts its share of bottom-feeders, flakes, and kooks. Fortunately, they are normally obvious and don't get very far.

Some people will stick to zine publishing in the same capacity as they did at fifteen years old. Many will apply these skills to other areas of their life and other interests. Most will fall somewhere in the middle.

Craven sums it up, "There was a time when, if somebody said, 'zines suck,' it meant they were squares who could only handle something nice, clean and acceptable to the masses. Now when somebody says, 'zines suck,' it means they don't care to read all about somebodies crushes or how they traveled from punk house to punk house." I would like to see the boundaries of zines expanded, not just for their audience's sake, but so more people would be interested in them as a medium for their own work.

We wish you success – on your own terms.

diy nike style: zines & the corporate world

By Stephen Duncombe

"Think! Think! It ain't illegal, yet!!" reads the first page of *U Don't Stop*, a zine I picked up the other day. It's not an unusual request.

Often hand-lettered, illustrated with cut and paste collages, and run off on photocopy machines, the message of the medium is that anyone can put one out. "The scruffier the better," argues Michael Carr, one of the editors of the punk zine *Ben is Dead*, because, "They look as if no corporation, big business or advertisers had anything to do with them." The anti-commercial ethos of the zine world is so commanding that writers who dare to move their project across the line into profitability—or at times even popularity—are reined in with the accusation of "selling out." In the shadows of capitalism, the zine world is busy creating a culture whose value isn't calculated as profit and loss on ruled ledger papers, but is assembled in the margins, using criteria like control, connection, and authenticity.

The search for authenticity drives the ethics of DIY. Against a world of pseudo-events and image consultants, zine writers are defining for themselves what's real. They use their zines to unleash an existential howl: I exist and here's what I think. *U Don't Stop* is a basketball zine; an intimate evocation of the street level scene which surrounds and sustains the game. Inside issue #2 there's a round up of the best public ball courts in Los Angeles, an interview with Munier, an African-American comic writer, and a tribute to the great funk musician George Clinton. B-ball related poetry and comics are salted throughout. *U Don't Stop*, like all zines, reads like a labor of love. One of the co-editors, Jimmy "Stank" Smith, sets the personal tone of the zine early with his hand scrawled introductory rant. In conventional scruffy zine style, with crossed off words kept in the text, he blasts out an impassioned plea for independent thought, ending his extemporaneous riff with the evocation: "Power." Indeed, it is a powerful testimonial of the irrepressible spirit of independent communication.

Well, maybe not. A little digging reveals that the two editors of *U Don't Stop*, Jimmy "Stank" Smith and John "Doc" Jay, are, in fact, copy writer and creative director, respectively, for the advertising firm of Wieden & Kennedy, the folks who sold sneakers to Gil Scott-Heron's "The Revolution Will Not Be Televised" and coined the famous DIY cry: "Just Do It!" Sure enough, the small print at the bottom of *U Don't Stop* reads ©1998 Nike Inc. This is DIY—Nike style.

Co-opting alternative culture, of course, is nothing new. Nike, adroit at strip-mining black youth culture for years, is actually a latecomer to the commercial harvest of the whiter alternative scene that zines represent. For years *Dirt* was a zine produced by the employees of the "Alternative Marketing" division of Warner records. The clothing chain Urban Outfitters churned out *Slant* (including a "punk rock" issue). The Body Shop printed up *Full Voice*, a zine lauding those who are "rebelling against a system that just won't listen" and encouraging others to do the same. Chris Dodge, professional librarian and zine bibliographer, estimates that there are dozens of these faux fanzines floating around out there.

What do corporations expect to reap in return from their zines? Not direct sales. Filled with the typical zine fare of rants, comics, interviews with musicians, and poetry, *U Don't Stop*—like most other astroturf zines—doesn't openly sell its patron's products. True, the street ball heroes of the zine's comic strip are wearing Nikes, and they've subsequently appeared on billboards in major urban markets, but this is low-key stuff. When I called Wieden & Kennedy's Jimmy Smith and asked him why the Nike logo was conspicuously absent from *U Don't Stop* he explained that, "The reason [the zine] is done without a swoosh is that kids are very sophisticated. It ain't like back in the day when you could do a commercial that showed a hammer hitting a brain: Pounding Headache. You know, it's gotta be something cool that they can get into." The goal is to create an association between the brand and "something cool they can get into," that is, a genuine grass-roots alternative culture. As David Rheins, former advertising director for SPIN Magazine, wrote in the trade journal *Mediaweek*, "It is not enough to merely package the right marketing message in a creative execution—it is necessary to deliver it in an environment that holds credibility with this audience." In more colloquial language Smith puts it this way: "If you've got them feeling you, you've won half the battle."

Advertisers, like zinesters, understand that commercial culture lacks authenticity. Built on instrumental market relationships—where people are considered a means to an end and not an end in themselves—capitalism is forever alienating the very individuals it relies upon to work, vote, and, in this case, buy. "Kids hate advertising," *U Don't Stop*'s Smith explain. "If they hate advertising and you're doing advertising, to me it sounds like you've got a little bit of a problem." Ironically, it's alternative culture like zines that offer a solution, providing a primary expression of people's lives and dreams: do-it-yourself authenticity. If properly packaged, the ideas, styles, and media of the underground provide material to renew and refresh the very culture they are created in opposition to. As *Business Week* reported in a special feature on new strategies in marketing, advertisers are now looking to "hide their corporate provenance." The report continues: "The idea is to fake an aura of colorful entrepreneurship as a way to connect with younger consumers who yearn for products that are hand-made, quirky, and authentic." An example *Business Week* offers of this fakery? No surprise: "mock 'zines'."

Many progressives—and zinesters—like to think of The System as a gray, pleasure-stomping behemoth. It is that. The rabble have to be kept in line and the best way to do this in a society where the jackboot is frowned on is to impose a uniform set of values and norms. The system is also something else: it's a consumer capitalist economy that depends on new ideas and new styles to open up new markets and sell more goods. "We track the movements among these progressive mind-sets," explains Janine Lopiano-Misdom and Joanne De Luca, co-founders of *The Sputnik Mindtrends Report* and authors of the recent <u>Street Trends: How Today's Alternative Cultures are Creating Tomorrow's Mainstream Markets</u>, "and interpret them into actionable opportunities for marketing, new product development, brand management and advertising." For the authors of <u>Street Trends</u>, anything and everything "progressive" becomes grist for the marketing mill, as chapter titles like "Positive Anarchy" and, you guessed it, "DIY: Do It Yourself," attest. In this environment, rebelling through culture means working as an unpaid intern for a market research firm.

But this sober realization needn't lead to a miserable fit of the blues. The dance continues, and faced with the discovery and commercialization of their culture, zine writers move on, some even poaching styles from the culture that stole from them. Carrie McLaren, for example, named her zine *Stay Free!*, pirating the name from a product that once promised women's liberation via the shining path of no-slide sanitary napkins. She's also picked up design tips from the slick, commercial magazines that Nike et al. are so desperate to distance themselves from. As Carrie points out, using a personal computer for desktop publishing means that it's actually easier to make her publication look "professional" than it is to replicate the old amateur aesthetic of zines. Besides, she adds, making her zine look nice means that more people will read what she has to say. This is important, for while the look of zines may be changing their message is not.

"I'm an asshole" reads the ad copy over a picture of a self-satisfied man showing off his sport utility vehicle on the back cover of *Stay Free!* #15, "And I've got the vehicle to prove it." From fake ads to interviews with media critics to a satirical quiz on how to "Test Your Book's Oprah Quotient" (Your protagonist is caught up in… A repressive political regime, -20 points; Problems at home, +50 points), *Stay Free!* mercilessly exposes, lampoons, and slaggs consumer culture from cover to cover. But in the spirit of DIY, the zine proposes something more: fighting the system. The tactic, however, that *Stay Free!* counsels is not retreat into some authentic subculture but moving out into the world, learning from the big boys, and employing the language and symbols that—for better or worse—constitute our lingua franca. Carrie and her friends, for example, staged a mock public salute to the Golden Marble children's advertising awards being held in New York City. Dressed as Goldie the Weasel, they handed out comic books "celebrating" the most egregious abuses of corporate America in their quest for the hearts and dollars of young people. As Carrie writes in her—carefully typeset—opening editorial in issue #14, "to fight a good fight you must access the enemy's power, and to see your own role in it, before deciding where to go from there."

Jean Railla, editor of the zine *Crafty Lady*, feels liberated by the direction that *Stay Free!* and her own—carefully crafted and digitally rendered—zine have gone, shifting emphasis away from preconceived style and toward what really matters: content and process. "It's not shocking to me that corporations are putting out fake zines. It makes total sense given the state of advertising in this culture."

"It used to make me sick; it was all the more reason to retreat into the subculture," Jean explains, acknowledging "this separatism really limited my scope and view of the world." "Now," she reflects, "I try to focus on saying what I want to say... and on the fact that girls out in the middle of Kansas still make zines for one another. The activity of making zines is what is really important— and all the marketing in the world cannot change that."

The left, like bohemia, has long held as an article of faith that certain stances, styles, and representations embody certain—progressive or conservative—politics. It's time to lose that religion. Sure, I'm disgusted by Nike's looting of my beloved zine culture, just as I shudder each time I hear "The Revolution Will Not Be Televised" as an ad jingle. But I also feel a curious sense of relief. The easy expropriation of even the most rebellious culture should open our eyes to the fact that pat notions about the "politics of representation," "cultures of resistance," and "authenticity" are hopelessly outdated. In our free-wheeling, postmodern playhouse of a world: Image is Nothing. No, wait, that's the ad copy for a Sprite commercial.

sustainability

I think you are at an advantage if you are *always* considering hanging up your projects. When I started my zine in 1992, I knew most zines lose plenty of money, and so I tried it for one year to see how things went. I continued to go through an intense soul-searching every four issues. It kept me sane, forced me to deal with the finances, and think about the big picture. The bargain I made with myself was that if I was (a) still enjoying what I was doing and (b) breaking even, or at least getting enjoyment relative to the degree of debt (c) chock full of fresh ideas for future issues – then I would keep doing the zine.

It's easy to get lazy, though. I think it's important to keep considering alternatives, like ways to keep down the cost (different printer, different printing technology, axing flaky distributors, printing fewer copies if I still have boxes of the last one sitting around) and ways to have more fun or at least to spread out the drudge work. For instance, I hated selling ads, although I was fairly good at it, so when I could afford to, I hired friends to help me with that. When I didn't have enough time to enter and fill orders, I trained others to do it. You have to ask for what you want. As you probably realize, most folks have no clue as to how much effort goes into a self-published project of any kind.

Typically, I was still in the hole from the previous issue when it came time to put up the cash for the next one. In my case, it was even more dangerous than for many folks because, as a thirty-something guy who had amassed a fair chunk of credit, I could always "just charge it."

For this reason, it is sometimes best to work on the small scale forever. Copying zines as you need them provides a financially feasible situation and you'll never have to move around boxes of zines! As Jackson elaborated on in the paper chapter, having a smaller number of copies that are read can be much more satisfying than a large print run being thrown away.

Sometimes what you really need is a break. Take a year or two off. All those people who've had real staying power in zine publishing have irregular schedules and sometimes put four years between issues. It's another way to take advantage of the adaptability of the medium.

Good reviews and positive feedback from readers can be very encouraging. This is supposed to be fun and you need to feel excited about doing your zine in order to keep doing it. Without inspiration, ultimately, your zine will reflect your negative feelings toward it.

Zines that make it to issue five tend to have a much more reliable future, which means that most zines don't make it past issue four. Making it to any number of issues is a success.

If you owe people money, do your best to pay them. You can usually work out a payment schedule, if you can't afford it all at once. Maybe you have a friend in the zine world who is willing to run ads and fill subscriptions in your stead. Sometimes you can fulfill your subscriber commitments by sending them other things. Just don't leave people hanging; it builds mistrust through the whole community and leaves people afraid to put dollar bills in envelopes. The zine world is surprisingly small in many ways, and the same people have a funny habit of showing up over and over in unfamiliar places. A bad reputation can dog you long after your project is laid to rest. So treat people with respect, and you will earn respect in return.

I know it sounds clichéd, but really, publishing your own work is its own reward. Have a blast, and may you use your creative power to achieve whatever success you desire.

The "Dead Magazines" issue of *Other magazine* celebrates the great magazines that have passed on. Articles include an inside look at *Punk Planet*, the original *Bitch* magazine and several magazine editors tell how DIY publishing ruined their lives. Anyone in the US can order *Other* #13 through www.Othermag.org.

appendices / resource lists

zine stores

33 1/3 Books
1200 N Alvarado Blvd. LA, CA 90026
52.5 Records
561 King St. Charleston, SC 29403
www.corporaterocksucks.com
Arise! Bookstore
2441 Lyndale Ave S Minneapolis, MN 55405
Artifacts: Good Books, Bad Art
202 Cascade Ave, Hood River, OR 97031
Atomic Books
1100 W. 36th St. Baltimore, MD 21211
www.atomicbooks.com
Axis Records & Comics
1431 A Park St Alameda, CA 94501
axisrecordsandcomics.com
The Beguiling
601 Markham St. Toronto, ON M6G 2L7
Big Brain Comics
1027 Washington Ave S Minneapolis, MN 55415
Big Idea Infoshop
724 Wood St. Wilkinsburg, PA 15221
Black Planet Radical & Anarchist Books
1621 Fleet St. Baltimore MD 21231

Black Rose Anarchist Bookshop
17a Lord St Newtown NSW 2042
Australia (02) 9519 9194
Bluestockings Bookstore
3817 5th Ave San Diego, CA 92103
Bluestockings Books
172 Allen St. New York, NY 10002
www.bluestockings.com
Bookwoman
918 W 12th St Austin, TX 78703
www.ebookwoman.com
Bound Together Books
1369 Haight St San Francisco, CA 94117
Boxcar Books
408 E 6th St. Bloomington, IN 47408
www.boxcarbooks.org
The Brian MacKenzie Infoshop
1426 9th St. NW Washington, DC 20001
www.dcinfoshop.org
Cherry Bomb Comics
41 New North Road, Eden Terrace, Auckland, New
Zealand (09) 374-4504 cherrybomb@ihug.co.nz
www.cherrybombcomics.co.nz
Cinders
103 Havemeyer St. Brooklyn, NY 11211

City Lights Books
261 Columbus Ave. San Francisco, CA 94133
www.citylights.com

Comic Relief
2138 University Ave., Berkeley, CA 94704
www.comicrelief.net

Comix Revolution
606 Davis St Evanston, IL 60201
(847) 866-8659

Cream City Collectives
732 E. Clarke St. Milwaukee, WI 53212

Criminal Records
466 Euclid Avenue Atlanta, GA 30307

Dog Eared Books
900 Valencia St San Francisco, CA 94110
(415) 282-1901 www.dogearedbooks.com

Domy Books
1709 Westheimer Houston, TX 77098
713-523-DOMY info@domystore.com
913 E Cesar Chavez Austin, TX 78704
512-476-DOMY (3669)

Earthlight Books
321 East Main St Walla Walla, WA 99362
1-866-630-4002 earthlightbooks@gmail.com

Elliot Bay Book Co.
1st S & S Main Seattle, WA 98104

End of An Ear
2209 South First St Austin TX 78704
(512) 462-6008

Fat Jack's Comicrypt
2006 Sansom St Philadelphia PA 19103-
4417 215-963-0788

Floating World Comics
20 NW 5th Ave #101, Portland, OR 97209

Flywheel Arts Collective
2 Holyoke St Easthampton, MA 01027
info@flywheelarts.org

Food Fight
1217 SE Stark St Portland, OR 97214
www.foodfightgrocery.com

Food for Thought Books
106 N Pleasant St. Amherst, MA 01002
www.foodforthoughtbooks.com

Forbidden Planet
840 Broadway NYC, NY 10003

Funny Papers
2025 Guadalupe #132 Austin TX 78705
(512) 478-9718 info@funnypapers.com

Giant Robot
2015 Sawtelle Blvd Los Angeles, CA 90025
618 Shrader Street San Francisco, CA 94117
437 E 9th St. New York, NY 10009
www.giantrobot.com

Global Aware
19 Kensington Ave. Toronto, ON M5T 2J8
www.globalaware.org 416-204-1984;

Ground Xero Records
1919 Northgate Blvd. Sarasota, FL 34234
www.groundxerorecords.com

Herbivore
1211 SE Stark Ave Portland, OR 97214
herbivoreclothing.com

Here
108 stokes croft / Bristol /bs1 3ru/ UK
http://www.slumberparty.co.uk/here/

House of the Rising Moon
207 E Meyers St Pittsburgh PA 15210

Hub Comics
19 Bow Street Somerville, MA 02143

In Other Words
8 NE Killingsworth St Portland, OR 97211
www.inotherwords.org

Internationalist Books
405 W Franklin St Chapel Hill, NC 27516-
2314 919-942-1740
http://www.internationalistbooks.org

Iron Rail Bookstore
511 Marigny St., New Orleans, LA 70117
www.ironrail.org

Irregular Rhythm Asylum
1-30-12-302 Shinjuku Shinjuku-ku, Tokyo
160-0022, Japan 03-3352-6916

Jim Hanley's Universe
4 West 33rd St, NYC 10001 (212) 268 7088 –
www.JHUniverse.com

Kustom Kulture
D-470 River Ave Winnipeg MB, R3L 0C8
204-453-7473

Last Word Books
211 4th Ave East Olympia, WA 98501
lastwordbooks(at)gmail.com 360-786-WORD
Laughing Horse Books
12 NE 10th St. Portland, OR 97232
(503)236-2893
Left Bank Books
92 Pike St. Seattle, WA 98101
www.leftbankbooks.com
Left Bank Books
399 N Euclid Ave St Louis, MO 63108
www.left-bank.com
Long Haul infoshop
3124 Shattuck Ave. Berkeley, CA 94705
www.thelonghaul.org
Lucy Parson's Center
549 Columbus Ave. Boston, MA 02118
www.lucyparsons.org
Magpie Magazine Gallery Inc.
1319 Commercial Dr Vancouver, BC V5L 3X5
May Day Books
301 Cedar Ave Minneapolis, MN 55454
www.maydaybookstore.org
May Day Books
155 1st Ave. Manhattan, NY 10003
www.maydaybooks.net
Meg Perry Center
644 Congress St Portland, ME 04101
info@peaceactionme.org
Meltdown Comics
7522 Sunset Blvd, LA, CA 90046
www.meltcomics.com
Minnesota Center for Book Arts
1011 Washington Ave S, Ste 100
Minneapolis, MN 55415 www.mnbookarts.org
The Misfit Theatre
335 Great North Road, Grey Lynn, Auckland,
1021, New Zealand.
the_misfit_theatre@hotmail.com
Missing Link
405 Bourke Street, Melbourne, 3000, Australia
Modern Times Bookstore
888 Valencia St. San Francisco, CA 94110
Mondragon

91 Albert Street, Winnipeg, MB Canada, R3B
1G5 http://mondragon.ca
Monkey Wrench Books
110 E North Loop Austin, TX 78751
www.monkeywrenchbooks.org
More Fun
105 East Main St Ashland, or 97520-1830
(541) 488-1978
Naked Eye
533 Haight St. San Francisco, CA 94117
Needles and Pens
3253 16th Ave. San Francisco, CA 94103
www.needles-pens.com
Off the Record
3849 5th Ave. San Diego, CA 92103
Open Books
4115 Barrancas Ave Pensacola, FL 32507
(850) 453-6774
Pages Bookstore
256 Queen St W Toronto, ON M6J 1E8 Canada
Park Ave CDs
2916 Corrine Drive Orlando, FL 32803
www.parkavecds.com
Pasture Music
705 East Johnson St. Madison, WI – 53703
608.441.1944
Polyester Books
330 Brunswick Street, Fitzroy, Victoria,
AUSTRALIA 3065 www.polyester.com.au/
Powell's Books
1005 W Burnside St. Portland, OR 97209
3723 SE Hawthorne Blvd Portland, OR 97214
503-228-4651, www.powells.com
Q is for Choir
2510 SE Clinton St. Portland, OR 97202
Quimby's
1854 W. North Ave. Chicago, IL 60622
www.quimbys.com
Rainbow Bookstore Cooperative
426 W Gilman Madison, WI 53703
rbc@supranet.net 608-257-6050
Reading Frenzy
921 SW Oak St. Portland, OR 97205
www.readingfrenzy.com

Red Emma's
800 Saint Paul St Baltimore, MD 21202
www.redemmas.org

Recycled Sounds
3941 Main St Kansas City, MO 64111

The Regulator Bookshop
720 Ninth St Durham, NC 27705 919-286-2700 http://www.regbook.com

Repo Man Records
Fensmarkgade 36
2200 København N Denmark

Rhino Records
235 Yale Ave Claremont, CA 91711
www.rhinorecords.cc

Rock Paper Scissors
2278 Telegraph Ave Oakland, CA 94612
www.rpscollective.com

A Room of One's Own Feminist Bookstore
307 W. Johnson St. Madison, WI 53703 Tel:
608-257-7888 Fax: 608-257-7457
room@chorus.net

Sandpaper Books
3706 N. Figueroa Ave. Los Angeles, CA 90065
www.florycanto.org

Sedition Books
4816 Old Spanish Trail Houston, TX 77021

Shake It Records
4156 Hamilton Ave. Cincinnati, OH 45223
www.shakeitrecords.com

Skylight Books
1818 N Vermont Ave Los Angeles, CA 90027
www.skylightbooks.com

Slacker
1321 Carson St. Pittsburgh, PA 15203

Star Clipper Comics
379 North Big Bend Blvd St Louis MO 63130
314-725-9110 www.starclipper.org

Sound on Sound
106 E North Loop Blvd Austin, TX 78751
(512) 371-9980

Spiral Objective
PO Box 126 Oaklands Park SA 5046 Australia
www.spiralobjective.com

The Stash
2213 S 1st St Austin, TX 78704
(512) 448-7707

Sticky
P.O.Box 310, Flinders Lane Post Office
Melbourne,Victoria 8009 Australia
sticky@platform.org.au

Stinkweed Records
1250 E. Apache #109 Tempe, AZ 85281

St. Mark's Bookshop
31 Third Ave. New York, NY 10003
www.stmarksbookshop.com

Sweet Hickory
317 East 3rd Bloomington, IN 47401
www.myspace.com/sweethickorymusicandart

33 1/3 Books
1200 N Alvarado Blvd. Los Angeles, CA 90026

Toronto Women's Bookstore
73 Harbord St Toronto, ON M5S 1G4, Canada
www.womensbookstore.com

Toxic Ranch
424 E 6th St Tucson, AZ 85705
www.toxicranchrecords.com

University Bookstore
TA Brady Commons Columbia, Mo. 65211
www.mubookstore.com

Vox Pop
1022 Cortelyou Rd Brooklyn 11218
(718) 940-2084
www.voxpopnet.com
308 Bowery New York, NY 10012
212.260.1600 (inside Bowery Poetry Club)

Waterloo
600 N Lamar Blvd # A Austin, TX 78703
(512) 474-2500

Wayward Council
807 W. University Ave Gainesville, FL 32601
wayward_council@yahoo.com

Wholly Craft
3171 N High St Columbus, OH 43202

Women and Children First
5233 N Clark St Chicago, IL 60640
www.womenandchildrenfirst.com

Wooden Shoe Books
508 S. Fifth Street Philadelphia, PA 19147
www.woodenshoebooks.com

zine distros

Active Distribution
BM ACTIVE, London, WC1N 3XX, England.
www.activedistribution.org
Long-running anarcho-punk distributor from London, England.

AK Press
674 A 23rd Ave. Oakland, CA 94612
www.akpress.org
Tens of thousands of titles mostly pertaining to radicalism and anarchism. They are hesitant to pick up low priced zines.

Approaching Apocalypse
Richmond, VA
approachingapocalypse@riseup.net
Dozens of titles focusing on political and social justice, punk, art, travel, how-to, anarchism,veganism, and dumpstering. Many titles are free. Wants submissions.

Arcade! Distro 4115 Still Glade Ln. Kingwood, TX 77345 www.arcadedistro.com

Personal, comic, DIY, vegan cookzines, and other fun stuff. Handed down several times.

Avocado Tree Distro
PO Box 2001 Abingdon, VA 24212
http://www.avocadotreedistro.com/
avocadotreedistro@gmail.com

Bikesexual distro
6131 Stafford Ave. Huntington Park, CA 90255

Black Book Press Distro
1608 Wilmette Ave Wilmette, IL 60091
Poetry.

Black Cat Distro
PO Box 229 Roberts Creek, BC V0N 2W0
http://users.resist.ca/~blackcat/Catalogue.print.pdf blackcat@resist.ca
A publisher, distributor, mailorder of anarchist goods

Black Panther distro
1876 Gilmore Ave. Winona, MN 55987
www.bpdistro.tk bpdistro@mail.com

Bottles On The Sill

2705 Great Forest Drive West Bend, WI 53090
bottlesonthesill@yahoo.com
www.geocities.com/bottlesonthesill/distro.html
Since spring 2004, they've distributed zines and buttons, homemade cards, original artwork, posters, and more. They're focused on trying to bring attention to under-appreciated zines, travel, teen, and arts and crafts. Looking for submissions.

C/S distro

Noemi Martinez PO box 621 Edinburg, TX
78540. csdistro@yahoo.com
www.csdistro.com
Zines from radical points of view, fresh approaches to parenting/mothering, color/culture, racism, culture, poverty, single parenting, parenting outside society's norm, trans issues, assault, mental health, DIY/cooking, herbs & wellness, crafts, as well as fiction, literary and poetry zines. Gives priority to Chicanas, mujeres and people of color.

Carrot Row

Dan Murphy PO Box 3154 Moscow ID 83843
An appreciator of things like gardening, plants, and quiet time.

Catastrophe Shop

PO Box 12299 St. Louis, MO 63157
www.usscatastrophe.com *Online diy comix shop. No longer accepting submissions.*

Click Clack

Nicole P.O. Box 35501 Richmond, VA 23235
New distro interested in large variety of zines, but nothing racist, homophobic, sexist, etc.

Dauntless Heart

39528 Atlanta Ave Zephyrhills, FL. 33540
www.geocities.com/dauntlessheart/

Dead Trees and Dye Distro

11 Glebe Way, Histon Cambridge, CB4 9HJ UK
deadtreesanddye@hotmail.com
A broad distro of zines and books from all over on a variety of topics, but with a strong focus on British titles.

Desert City Death Distro

81 W. Lewis Phoenix, AZ 85003
http://www.desertcitydeathdistro.150m.com
Features a number of zines not available elsewhere.

Else Joffi

http://www.else-joffi.de/
An earnest zine distro from Germany.

Fall of Autumn

Alan, Aaron, & Kate PO Box 254 Manhattan,
IL 60442 www.fallofautumn.com
Pioneer of the zinester podcast readings, filmstrips, news articles, a distro, and some future publishing projects.

Firestarter Press

PO Box 50217 Baltimore, MD 21211
firestarter@riseup.net

Fretless Distro

Tampa, FL inertialily@gmail.com

Frostbite Distro

Minneapolis, MN
http://www.myspace.com/frostbitedistro

Gigglebot Distro

Jessaruh 1990 Rocksram Drive Buford, GA
30519 www.gigglebot.net

Gimme Brains!!! Distro

San Francisco www.youreinsanehoney.com
youreinsanehoney@gmail.com

Global Hobo

PO Box 170447 San Francisco CA 94117-0447
www.hobocomics.com
Mini-Comix based distributor of cool hand made goods.

Glow Dome Distro
www.northwestofthenation.com/glowdome/d
omemain.html
*A mobile Airstream trailer with a traveling
craft and zine distro!*

Great Worm Express Distribution
PO box 19013 360A Bloor ST. West Toronto,
ON M5S 3C9 CANADA www.greatworm.ca
*Frandroid's main mission is to go through tons of
crappy zines so that you don't have to. What you
get in the end is the best zines out there, featured
on the Great Worm website. You'll find zines about
politics, sexuality, punk rock, food, cinema, comics,
humor, urban exploration and motherhood.*

In Our Hearts
123 Tompkins Brooklyn, NY 11206 718-404-9319
www.123communityspace.org
*A zine distro, community lending library,
infoshop storefront, and after school program
for neighborhood youngsters!*

Kersplebedeb
PO Box 63509 CCCP Van Horne, Montreal, QC
H3W3H8 Canada. 514 735 3721
www.kersplebedeb.com
*An anarchist mailorder, publisher of radical
books, buttons, zines & pamphlets, and
manufacturer of radical agit prop matarials. Huge
catalog.*

Ladymen
Stephanie B PO Box 1211 New York, NY
10029-9998 www.ladymen.8m.com/

Last Gasp
777 Florida St. San Francisco, CA 94110
415-824-6636 www.lastgasp.com
*Since 1970, Last Gasp has been distributing and
publishing staunchly independent comics and zines.
They have carved out a niche of distributing to non-
trade stores as a place that will reliably have a good
selection of edge literature.*

Learning To Leave A Paper Trail Distro
Ciara Xyerra PO Box 100, Medford, MA 02153
learningtoleaveapapertrail@hotmail.com
http://papertrail.zinetastic.com
*Storytelling zines, fiction, DIY guides, radical
history projects, reproductive health manuals,
mama's politico writings, cut & paste, punk
rock travel tales, anti-oppression stuff,
sustainable living tips, & more! The distro
opened in October 2003 & accepts zines for
consideration that generally fit into something
resembling the above descriptions.*

Lick My Lit
www.freewebs.com/lickmylit
*"I want this distro to feature zines, spoken
word, underground film, and music by people
whom I consider to be good friends or those who
submit a zine that I feel a real connection too. "*

Lilmag
Momo Nonaka 15-2-307, Chuo Nakano-ku,
Tokyo 164-0011 Japan http://lilmag.org *A
very cute Japanese distributor of zines and
related materials.*

Loop Distro
billy the bunny 1357 W. Augusta #1/Chicago,
IL 60622 zines@fastworks.com
www.loopdistro.com
*Chicago-based zine distro that has been around
since 2002. Lots of personal zines, comics,
books, CD's, and other random junk, most of
which is from Chicago or the Midwest. They
accept submissions.*

Love Life! Distro
www.freewebs.com/lovelifedistro/

Lunacy Distro
c/o the Long Haul Info Shop 3124 Shattuck
Ave Berkeley, CA 94705
www.radicalmentalhealth.net
lunacydistro@riseup.net
Zines focused around mental health issues.

Marching Stars
www.marchingstars.co.uk

mnm distro
http://mnm.xrea.jp/distro/

Microcosm Publishing and Distribution
222 S Rogers St. Bloomington, IN 47404
www.microcosmpublishing.com
*Zines, books, pamphlets, stickers, buttons,
patches, t-shirts, posters, films, and more!
Hopes to add credibility to zine writers and
their ethics, teach self empowerment, show
hidden history, and nurture people's creative
side. Catalog is $1.*

Northstardistro
Kelly Beliveau #18 4131 lakeshore rd
kelowna, bc v1w 1v8 canada
kellybeliveau@hotmail.com
http://northstar.dime-a-dozen.net
*Kelly carries personal (especially themed personal)
and literary zines, and always accepts submissions.
She is trying to distribute some of the lesser known,
yet equally talented zinesters' work.*

NOVA RECORDINGS
Vincenzstr. 24/26 51065 Koeln Germany
http://novarecordings.net *A German Record
Label/mailorder that also stocks some choice
personal zines and related items.*

Not Sorry Distro
http://www.notsorry.org/
*A distro focusing around body, size, gender,
and identity politics from Portland, OR.*

Overground Distro
Chicago, IL http://www.overground.info
*Anarchist distributor of pamphlets and
personal is political zines.*

Parcell Press
P.O. Box 14647 Richmond, VA 23221
www.parcellpress.com/
*"Contrary to unpopular belief, Parcell Press is
neither a machine nor a team. It's just me, Taylor,
hanging out in a second floor apartment office,
sifting through crates of zines and boxes of mail on
a daily basis, plugging away on this computer and
scribbling things onto pieces of paper that usually
get lost beneath other pieces of paper."*

Planting Seeds Press
PO Box 54 Franklin Square, NY 11010-0054
www.plantingseedspress.com/

PXS Distro
www.pxsdistro.com/

Radical Rabbit
Luke Romano 101B Cooper St. Westmont, NJ 08108
http://www.freewebs.com/radicalrabbitdistro/
Anti-authoritarian music & zines

Riveter Distro
412 W. Church St. #2 Champaign, IL 61820
www.angelfire.com/hi5/riveter/
A radical feminist distro with unique titles.

Slumgullion Bicycle Powered Distro
235 North First Street, Missoula MT 59802
http://www.slumgullion.org/
*A co-op distro partnered with an artists center
that has a mobile bicycle unit to sell zines
around town!*

Smallzone
Shane Chebsey 10 Cleveland Ave, High Ercall,
Telford, Shropshire TF6 6AH. UK
chebbo@aol.com www.smallzone.co.uk
*All self published reading material in various
languages from many countries.. They sell to most
countries. Submit via website.*

South Chicago Anarchist Black Cross Distro
P.O. Box 721 / Homewood, IL 60430

Dozens of anarchist prisoner zines and related materials.

Starfiend Distro
904-939 Homer St / Vancouver, BC V6B 2W6
jenn@starfiend.com www.starfiend.com
A long-running distro that stacks a wide breadth and substantial catalog.

Starting Small
Missy Kulik PO Box 8062 Athens, GA 30603
www.missykulik.com
Carries zines and comics by Missy and friends. Titles such as "Where's a Cookie?", "Dork Lifestyle", "Pearshaped", and "Catch That Beat!". Cute handmade items such as necklaces, charms, and sock monkeys, plus zine gift bags!

Static Cling Distro
po box 20083 rpo beverly edmonton, ab canada t5w 5e6
www.freewebs.com/static_cling/
An extensive distro with plans to donate all profits to charity.

Stickfigure
PO box 55462 Atlanta, GA 30308
info@stickfiguredistro.com
www.stickfiguredistro.com
Open to all sorts of zines, but quality is a must.

Stitchy Press
Drumnadubber Drumsna Drumsna, County Leitrim IE Ireland stitchypress@gmail.com

Stranger Danger Zine Distro
2236 n. sawyer ave. #1 Chicago, IL 60647
www.strangerdangerdistro.com
Interested in zines of a personal manner that focus on queer/fat/trans positivity as well as other subjects. Submissions are welcome.

Sweet Candy distro
Sage P.O. Box 1833 Dallas, GA 30132
sage@eyecandyzine.comwww.eyecandyzine.com
Take a stroll through Sweet Candy and take a look at what they already carry to see the wide variety they're interested in stocking. Art, poetry, perzines, compilation projects, food/vegan zines. As well as DIY paper items, buttons, music, artwork, and more.

Tarantula Distro
818 SW 3rd Ave. PMB #1237 Portland, OR 97204
tarantula@socialwar.net www.socialwar.net
Anarchist academic distro that distributes and republishes classic texts.

Transcendent
www.transcendentonline.com
transcendent_online@yahoo.com

Tree of Knowledge
Mary Chamberlin PO Box 251766, Little Rock, AR 72225
In the early '90s, Theo Witsell, back from a stint in Atlanta, starts a book and zine distro in the back room of his house during shows. It explodes in popularity in the next few years, thanks in no small part to frequent tabling at fests around the country, and the fact that people believe in mailorder. It blew into something larger around the year 2000.

Wasabi Distro
Andrea Hope MBE 147, Akasaka Twin Towers, 2-17-22 Akasaka, Minato-ku, Tokyo 107-0052
info@wasabi-distro.com http://www.wasabi-distro.com
Zines in English, Japanese, and Korean. Willing to accept submissions of just about anything, in any language, with the only exceptions being porn and erotica.

Whammy Industries
Stephanie Scarborough P. O. Box 981 Fort Worth, TX 76101 ww.atomicglee.com/whammy
A strong focus on food and cooking centric zines and related goods.

zine libraries

56A Infoshop, 56 Cramptpn Street, London SE17 3AE, England. www.safetycat.org/56a

ABC no RIO, 156 Riverton St., NYC 10002 www.abcnorio.org/facilities/zine_library.html

Aboveground Zine Library 511 Marigny St. New Orleans, LA 70117 Abovegroundlibrary@yahoo.com or 504-944-0366 Open Sun thru Sat from 1 to 7 pm

Alternative Media Library c/o Michelle Chen PO Box 200077 New Haven, CT 06520

Anchor Archive Zine 5684 Roberts St Halifax, Nova Scotia B3K 1J6 Canada 902-446-1788 anchorarchive@gmail.com http://anchor.revolt.org

Anno Domini Zine Library, 150 S. Montgomery St.Unit B, San Jose CA 95110; 408-271-5151; www.galleryAD.com; open M-Th "*We accept zines of all types and formats but focus on the creative and artistic type of zines (vs. the rant type). We'd like the collection to invoke a creative spirit that inspires others to express themselves.*"

AS A WHOLE "Alternative Culture, Art Resource Center" asawhole_family@yahoo.com #386 Makiling St. (Lower) Central Park Subd. Bangkal, Davao City Philippines 8000 Philippines *You can help us through donations.*

Asian American Zine Archive, c/o Darrell Y. Hamamoto, Asian American Studies Program, 3102 Hart Hall, University of California—Davis, Davis, CA 95616; 530-752-5600; by appointment only. *Asian American Zine Archive at the University of California, Davis is the only repository of its kind that specializes in written and graphic expression produced by Asian Americans who either by choice or default circumvent corporate-controlled monopoly communication outlets.*

Austin Zine Library, 300 Allen St., Austin TX 78702; www.geocities.com/theaustinzinelibrary; austinzinelibrary@yahoo.com; *drop-in: inside*

the Rhizome Collective, in the back warehouse, in the back left corner, across from the Food Not Bombs kitchen; open Su, Tu *"The Austin Zine Library is a new organization, to provide zine-lovers and other curious folks a place where they can come and read underground literature they might not be able to find anywhere else. We have about 1,500 zines, and are always looking for more."* Seeking volunteers.

Baltimore County Public Library Zine Collection 9833 Greenside Dr Cockeysville, Maryland 21030-2188 410-887-7750 www.bcpl.info/centers/library/zines.html

Barnard College Library 3009 Broadway, New York, NY 10027 jfreedma@barnard.edu www.barnard.edu/library/zines/index.htm

Batt Annex Center for Learning and Resources, 3024 Minnehaha Ave., Minneapolis MN 55404; 612-724-2161; open W-Th, Sa *Offers a resource center, a library, meeting space, and classes on self-empowerment.*

Bibliograph/e Zine Library (inside Toc Toc Cafe) 6091 Avenue du Parc Montreal, QC H2V 2K7

Booklyn / Attn: Emily / Zine 37 Greenpoint Ave, 4th Fl Brooklyn, NY 11222

Bottles On The Sill Jessica Bublitz 2705 Great Forest Drive West Bend, WI 53090 USA bottlesonthesill@yahoo.com http://www.geocities.com/bottlesonthesill/distro.html.

Bread and Roses Library at CAMP, 3022 Cherokee, St. Louis, MO 63163. www.stlcamp.org

Carnegie Library of Pittsburgh – Teens, 4400 Forbes Ave. Pittsburgh, PA 15213

wilkj@carnegielibrary.org 412-622-3121 *Category-based browsing collection and happily accept donations. The Mr. Roboto Project's zine library is defunct and it is being consolidated into our public library collection.*

Charm City Art Space Jessee Maloney 4820 Roland Ave. Apt B Baltimore, MD 21210

Che Cafe Zine Library, 9500 Gilman Dr., Student Center B-0323C, La Jolla CA 92093 858-534-2311 zinelibrary@checafe.ucsd.edu checafe.ucsd .edu/zines.html; open during events or by appointment *"The Che Cafe is a community space and resource center for radical grassroots activists. The Che is most interested in zines addressing political and social issues, rather than personal dialogues and poetry; especially looking for DIY how-to guides."* See website for information to include with donated zines.

Civic Media Center, 1021 W. University Ave, Gainesville, FL 32601. www.civicmediacenter.org

Cleveland Public Library 17133 Lakeshore Blvd Cleveland, OH 44110 adiamond@cpl.org *Housed in the Popular Library, the collection of zines by local authors expanded to include hundreds of zines from across the United States. Zines circulate for three weeks Accepts donations of zines related to Ohio and written by Clevelanders.*

Darby Romeo Collection of Zines (Collection 168), attn: Julie Graham, Special Collections Librarian, UCLA Arts Library Special Collections, Young Research Library, Room 22478, Los Angeles CA 90095-1575; 310-825-7253; open M-F by appointment only *"We accept any zine as long as it doesn't contain any perishable materials (e.g. food). Due to space limitations we cannot accept multiple copies of a single issue. Collection consists of privately printed and distributed arts and literary magazines."*

Denver Zine Library 1644 Platte Street / Denver CO 80202 Mailing address: PO Box 13826 / Denver, CO 80201 http://www.denverzinelibrary.org dzl@denverzinelibrary.org

The Dry River Radical Resource Center, *c/o Skrappys, 201 E. Broadway, Tucson AZ 85701-2013; open Tu and Th "A consensus-based, non-hierarchical collective works out of the space to bring anarchy to Arizona, with such features as a fairly extensive zine library and a clothes closet. All zines are welcome, there is no particular focus, save perhaps a focus on practicality/diy projects."*

Durland Alternatives Library, 127 Anabel Taylor Hall, Cornell University, Ithica NY 14853; 607-255-6486; alt-lib@cornell.edu; www.alternativeslibrary.org *"We collect progressive political, alternative health, human rights and prison issues, homeschooling, ecology, and more—we try to offer zines that are not available in other places in town. We are also interested in viewpoints not expressed in mainstream media sources and look for information that is getting harder and harder to find."*

Evergreen Infoshoppe, The Evergreen State College, Student Activities, CAB 320, Olympia WA 98505; 360-867-5114; evergreeninforshoppe@yahoo.com; hours subject to volunteer availability *"The infoshoppe accepts all zine donations for its library, but especially wants submissions from students, locals, and alumni. ... We aim to spread awareness of campus groups, establish a central community calendar and bulletin board, and help fund individual zine projects."*

The Flying Brick Library and Reading Room, PO Box 5021, Richmond VA 23220, attn: Greg Wells; 804-644-2544; gregwells36@hotmail.com; drop-in: 506 S. Pine St., Richmond VA 23220, *call first "The Flying Brick Library and Reading Room is a small radical resource library based in the front room of a collectively owned household of anarchists. We ... have a collection that includes 2,000 books available for checkout as well as 1,500 periodicals, 500 zines and pamphlets, comics and file folders covering a wide range of national and local political and social issues. We are always looking for new zines that deal with political, social, and personal issues."*

Flywheel Zine Library, 2 Holyoke Street, Easthampton, MA 01027. www.flywheelart.org

Independent Publishing Resource Center, 917 SW Oak #218, Portland, OR 97205. www.iprc.org *"Since its inception in 1998 the center has been dedicated to encouraging the growth of a visual and literary publishing community by offering a space to gather and exchange information and ideas, as well as to produce work. The IPRC is an Oregon 501(c)(3) Nonprofit organization."*

Knight Library Special Collections, 1299 University of Oregon, Eugene OR 97403-1299, attn: James Fox; *open M-Sa Collecting primarily Northwest, US zines: N. California to British Columbia, Alaska, Idaho, Montana, Nevada. All zines are welcome, any genre. Once cataloged, everyone will have access. All zines will be listed/described in an online database eventually.*

Labadie Collection, 711 Harlan Hatcher Library, University of Michigan, Ann Arbor MI 48109; attn: Julie Herrada; 734-764-9377; jherrada@umich.edu; www.lib.umich.edu/spec-coll/labadie; open M-Sa *Primarily interested in anarchist-leaning publications. "We still collect anarchist zines, but also the not-explicitly-anarchist-but-with-anarchist-leanings like anti-tech, radical environmental, animal liberation, alternative energies and economies, DIY, critical mass, etc., and zines written by and about transgender, especially trans-youth."*

The Little Maga/Zine Collection, Book Arts & Special Collections, San Francisco Public Library, 100 Larkin Street, San Francisco CA 94102, attn: Andrea Grimes; 415-557-4560; agrimes@sfpl.org; www.sfpl.org/librarylocations/main/bookarts /zines/zines.htm; *open Tu-Su Little magazines and zines are collected, with special emphasis on the San Francisco experience. More than 1000 in collection; titles cataloged on website.*

Long Haul Infoshop, 3124 Shattuck, Berkeley CA 94705; 510-540-0751; www.thelonghaul.org; open Su-Th *"We are primarily an activist center and community space. We do have an extensive radical periodical collection spanning the past couple of decades. Anarchist and radical zines encouraged. If you're donating a zine, please indicate that it's a donation for the library/infoshop."*

Madison Infoshop, 1019 Williamson, Madison WI 53703; 608-262-9036; www.madisoninfoshop.org; open M-F *"We're a volunteer-run resource center available to the Madison and UW community. We're a community space offering a range of resources including, but not limited to, books, magazines, videos, and topic files, from an activist perspective."*

Mansfield Library, Small Press Collection, University of Montana, Missoula MT 59812, attn: Chris Mullin; open Su-F *"We want one copy of every zine we can get, and will try to keep that copy safe forever, but anybody can read it whenever we're open. The only reason we keep these locked up, and make the photocopies ourselves, is so that they will still be around 50 or 100 years from now. Send them along! We have close to 2,000 issues."*

May Day Infoshop, 155 First Ave., New York NY 10003; www.maydaybooks.net; *open daily "(We are) committed to providing the working class with resources that will assist their efforts to understand and transform the world. We distribute a variety of books, periodicals, pamphlets, audio and video tapes, and other educational materials on contemporary political, economic, and social issues through our bookstore and lending library."*

Michigan State University Libraries, 100 Library, Michigan State University, East Lansing MI 48824-1048, attn: Randall W. Scott, Popular Culture Bibliographer; 517 355-3770; scottr@msu.edu; www.lib.msu.edu/comics; open daily *"We are accepting zines, and though we focus our cataloging efforts on comix ones, all are welcome. The zines are not kept separate in our collection but cataloged using the Library of Congress system. Cataloging is slow but sure: nothing is disrespected or thrown away."*

Minneapolis Technical College, Library Zine Collection, 1501 Hennepin Ave, Minneapolis, MN 55403

Multnomah County Public Library Portland, OR www.multcolib.org/books/zines/ *Available at Belmont, Central, Hillsdale, Holgate, Hollywood, Midland, North Portland, Northwest, and Sellwood-Moreland libraries. Zines on many subjects are available, from personal stories to zines about cooking, work, politics, typewriters, health, and more. Wants to pay for your zines. Does not accept donations.*

Olympia Zine Library, c/o Last Word Books, 119 5th Ave. SE, Olympia WA 98501; 360-357-5255; open M-Sa *"The bulk of the collection is made up of music, punk, political, personal, and riot grrrl zines. We accept all zine donations."*

Papercut 45 Mt. Auburn St. Cambridge, MA 02138 papercut@riseup.net. www.papercutzinelibrary.org *A free lending library that operates out of the Democracy Center in Harvard Square. Its circulating collection includes over 7,000 titles, on a wide* range of topics and formats.

Paperfort 222 S Rogers St. Bloomington, IN 47404 www.librarything.com/profile/paper.fort *Rapidly growing zine library housed inside Rhino's Youth Center, 331 S Walnut St*

People's Free Space 144 Cumberland Ave. Portland, ME 04101, 207-822-9869, www.peoplesfreespace.org *They have a lending library, kids space, free room, offices, computers, kitchen, books and zines for sale and a common room for workshops, performances, meetings and events. Food Not Bombs, Portland Tenants Union and GE Free Maine all work out of the space, and other community groups such as the Portland Victory Gardens Project and the Winter Cache Project meet and hold events there.*

PNCA Library Zine Collection 1241 NW Johnson St. Portland, OR 97219 *Accepts any style, size, and genre. and welcome minicomics, chapbooks, and other handmade books in addition to zines. All items are cataloged (and therefore searchable in the library catalog on campus and online at http://library.pnca.edu) and kept in a permanent collection. Distros are also encouraged to send us catalogs for us to order from.* Email rachel@pnca.edu with questions.

Popular Culture Library William T Jerome Library Bowling Green St. Univ. Bowling Green, OH 43403

Purchase College Zine Library, 735 Anderson Hill Rd. #1333, Purchase NY 10577, attn: Alisa Richter; culturevulture7@aol.com

Queen Zine Library 95 The Country Way, Kitchener, Ontario N2E 2K3 Canada queenzine@hotmail.com www.livejournal.com/users/queenzine *All donations are eligible for feature in the QZ Newsletter which is irregularly published and features excerpts from the newest zines the library has received.*

Queer Zine Archive Project, 2935 N. Fratney, Milwaukee WI 53212; www.qzap.org; qzap@qzap.org *"The mission of the Queer Zine Archive Project (QZAP) is to establish a "living history" archive of past and present queer zines and to encourage current and emerging zine publishers to continue to create." Collection is online only; collects all queer zines of all formats (print and digital).*

Salt Lake City Public Library Zine Collection, 209 E 500 S., Salt Lake City, UT 84111. www.slcpl.lib.ut.us

Santa Cruz Anarchist Infoshop, 509 Broadway, Santa Cruz CA 95060-4621; open daily *This new infoshop houses a huge anarchist lending library, a giant zine collection, free tea, amazing people, soon-to-be free public internet access and computer publishing access, and much more.*

Sedition Books Info Shop http://houston.indymedia.org/news/2007/02/56554.php *After being ravaged by a recent fire, believed to be arson, Sedition is presently seeking a new commercial space. Donations may be sent c/o The Alarm P O Box 66362 Houston, TX 77266-7614*

Sheridan Zine Library Jen Pilles 491 Lakeshore Road West Oakville, ON L6K 1G4

Sin Reading Room at the Firebrand collective www.thefirebrand.org/sin 918 Ward St., *East Nashville after 5 PM and weekends.*

Solidarity! Revolutionary Center and Radical Library 1119 Massachusetts St Lawrence, KS 66044

Stonewall Library & Archives, 1717 N. Andrews Ave., Ft. Lauderdale FL 33311; 954-763-8565; info@stonewall-library.org; www.stonewall-library.org *"Our mission is to collect, preserve, organize for use, and display materials relating to gay, lesbian, bisexual,* *and transgender culture and history." Contact before donating.*

Sweet Candy Zine Library Sage P.O. Box 1833 Dallas, GA 30132 *Voted Philly's Punkest Zine Library 2006 Presently on hiatus.*

Thomas J. Dodd Research Center, University of Connecticut, Archives and Special Collections, 405 Babbidge Rd., Unit 1205, Storrs CT 06269-1205; 860-486-4500; www.lib.uconn.edu/online/research/speclib/AS C *The Alternative Press Collections contains comics and fanzines. Their collection of comics consists of over 70 titles. Fanzines, collected from the United States and Western Europe, are primarily science fiction and fantasy.*

Toronto Zine Library Located at: TRANZAC 292 Brunswick Avenue, south of Bloor Second Floor Rehersal Hall Mon-Fri- 5pm-close Sat and Sun- 1pm-close *Donations*: TZL c/o Tara Bursey 68 Crawford St Toronto, Ontario M6J 2V2 torontozinelibrary@hotmail.com sitekreator.com/zinelibrary/index.html

University of Kentucky Zine Archive
www.uky.edu/Libraries/index.php *In 2006 it was determined that few organizations in the southern region collected zines and that a centralized repository should be established at UK. Additionally, zine publications represent a vastly undocumented portion of society and without actively pursuing these materials that information would be lost. Mon-Fr 8-5. A keyword searchable database is available through http://kdl.kyvl.org. Print zines related to gender issues, politics, the environment, Appalachian studies, and popular or alternative culture. We are requesting donations of single issues as well as large collections*

Urbana-Champaign Independent media Center
218 W. Main Street, Suite 110 Urbana, IL 61801 librarians@ucimc.org

Warehouse 21, 1614 Paseo de Peralta, Santa Fe NM 87501; 505-989-4423; www.warehouse21.org; open M-F *"W21 kindly receives zines in art, poetry, politics and social issues."*

West Coast Zine Collection, Special Collections and University Archives, Library and Information Access, San Diego State University, 5500 Campanile Dr., San Diego CA 92182-8050; infodome.sdsu.edu/about/depts/spcollections/r arebooks/zinesfindingaid.shtml *"An archive of West Coast zines and comics. Zines in this collection will not circulate beyond the library but anyone can use the Archive. We are collecting all zines related to gender and gender issues, music, art, and popular and alternative culture." Focuses on publications west of the Mississippi and south of the U.S.-Mexico Border.*

Wisconsin Historical Society Attn: James Danky 816 State Street Madison, Wisconsin 53706-1482 James Danky, Newspapers and Periodicals Librarian (608)264-6598 jpdanky@whs.wisc.edu

The Women's Library Old Castle Street, London E1 7NT UK Telephone +44 (0)20 7320 2222; Fax +44 (0)20 7320 2333; enquirydesk@thewomenslibrary.ac.uk *Our zines reflect women's experiences in the UK. Further details about them can be found at* www.thewomenslibrary.ac.uk/cat_zine.html

Zine and Publishing Project (ZAPP),
Richard Hugo House, 1634 11th Ave, Seattle, WA 98122. zines@hugohouse.org *One of the coolest, best hang-outs in Seattle with over 10,000 titles in their collection.*

Zine Librarians Discussion List
http://groups.yahoo.com/group/zinelibrarians

For more information about zine libraries (starting, running, and locating them) contact zinelibrarian@yahoo.com

zine reviewers

Almost Normal Comics, members.tripod.com/almostnormalcomics/id 181.htm. Send items to PO Box 12822, Ft. Huachuca AZ 85670, flesh_on_bone@yahoo.com

Alternative Press Review *prints lots of reviews, including excerpts. Quarterly.* Box 4710, Arlington VA 22204, www.altpr.org, editors@altpr.org ($3)

Broken Pencil *mostly covers Canadian zines, but has American zines as well, plus excellent articles/reprints on zines, publishing, and other nifty topics. Quarterly.* PO Box 203, Stn P, Toronto, ON M5S 2S7 Canada, www.brokenpencil.com, editor@brokenpencil.com ($5.95)

Comics Journal, *comics only.* 7563 Lake City Way NE, Seattle WA 98115, www.tcj.com, $6

Factsheet 5: *Check website to see if they ever start publishing again.* PO Box 4660, Arlington VA 22204, www.factsheet5.org, deanthomas@comcast.net.

Fall of Autumn PO Box 254 Manhattan, IL 60442 www.fallofautumn.com

Feminist Review PO Box 1683 Athens, GA 30603 www.feminist-review.com

410 Media 1204 S. MacArthur Blvd. Springfield, IL 62704 410Media.com

The Free Press Death Ship, *lots of reviews and excerpts. Will not review items containing ISBN.* Violet Jones, PO Box 55336, Hayward CA 94545 *(free/donations accepted)*

Hanging Like a Hex Ryan Canavan 201 Maple Lane N. Syracuse, NY 13212 www.hanginghex.com

Give Me Back PO Box 73691 Washington, DC 20056 www.givemeback.org *The new rebirth of HeartattaCk zine!*

Last Hours PO Box 382 456- 458 The Strand London WC2R OD2 UK www.lasthours.org.uk

Livejournal, www.livejournal.com/community/zinereviews

MaximumRockNRoll, *especially punk zines. Published monthly.* PO Box 460760, San Francisco CA 94146 ($3)

New Pages Zine Rack – www.newpages.com/magazinestand/zines/default.htm. ZineRack – NewPages, PO Box 726, Alpena, MI 49707.

Poopsheet, www.poopsheetfoundation.com Rick Bradford, PO Box 2235, Fredericksburg TX 78624

Profane Existence PO Box 8722 Minneapolis, MN 55408 www.profaneexistence.com

Razorcake PO Box 42129 Los Angeles, CA 90042 www.razorcake.org

Rocktober 1507 E. 53rd St. #617 Chicago, IL 60615 www.roctober.com/

Slug & Lettuce, *especially punk zines.* Chris Boarts, PO Box 26632, Richmond VA 23261 (55¢ stamp)

Syndicated Reviews http://syndicatedzinereviews.blogspot.com

Xeroxography Debt, *the review zine with latent per-zine tendencies. Thrice Annually.* Davida Gypsy Breier, PO Box 963, Havre de Grace MD 21078, davida@leekinginc.com, www.leekinginc.com/xeroxdebt ($3)

Zinethug, Marc Parker, 2000 NE 42 Ave #221, Portland OR 97213 www.zinethug.com

Zinetopia, Sarah Arrr! PO Box 235 North Tazewell, VA 24630 piratesarah@gmail.com http://zinetopia.wordpress.com/

Zine World is *published once a year.* PO Box 330156, Murfreesboro TN 37133-0156, jerianne@undergroundpress.org, www.undergroundpress.org *($4)*

ZUM!'s Comix Review Distribution List, *"The purpose of the ZUM! Reviews List is to distribute new reviews of comix to its subscriber." Reviews archived on website.* list.zetnet.co.uk/mailman/listinfo/reviews

What you will likely notice is that the reviewers section is much shorter than libraries, distros, or stores. In the last few years the zine community has lost many zine reviewers and publications. Even some of the ones listed here are on extended hiatus. Some of the reason for this is that publishing and distributing magazines became much more difficult and multiple companies went bankrupt. This is an excellent void to fill with some new energy and different approaches! Bonus points for new methods and new distribution models!

zine events

Allied Media Conference is in June at Wayne State University in Detroit. It has been running for ten years. Tools and tactics for transforming our communities through media-based organizing. PO Box 442339, Detroit MI 48232. www.alliedmediaconference.org

Alternative Press Expo is held in November in San Francisco. Over 300 exhibitors and 4,800 attendees in 2007, APE features an incredible gathering of indy, alternative, and self-published comics, books, and zines. www.comic-con.org/ape/

Boston Zine Party www.bostonzinefair.org

Canzine Canada's biggest zine fair, in Toronto & a second satellite city. www.brokenpencil/canzine

Chicago zine event in May @ Museum of Contemporary Art. Sponsored by Quimbys.

Denver Zine Fest is in May. www.denverzinefest.com

Ephemera Festival is in May in Chicago. http://michelleaiello.googlepages.com/ephemerafestival

Expozine (in Montréal) www.expozine.ca

FLUKE Mini Comix—Zine Explosion (Athens, Ga.), www.flukeathens.com

Houston Zine Fest is in May. www.myspace.com/zinefesthouston

London Zine Symposium is put on by *Last Hours* in England each April. www.londonzinesymposium.org.uk

Madison Zine Fest http://www.madisonzinefest.org, www.midwestzines.org

Manchester Zine Fest www.manchesterzinefest.org.uk/

Milwaukee Zine Fest is in July. www.midwestzines.org/5.html.

MoCCA is in June and features huge attendance in Manhattan. www.moccany.org

Montréal Anarchist Bookfair each year in May www.anarchistbookfair.ca/en/

New Jersey Zinefest is in April at Rutgers in New Brunswick. Free pizza, a vegan bake sale, and an open mic!

New Orleans Bookfair:
www.hotironpress.com/bookfair.htm

New York Anarchist Bookfair
anarchistbookfair.net

North of Nowhere Expo. organized by Edmonton Small Press Association in October www.edmontonsmallpress.org/nonexpo.html.

Olympia Zine Gathering/Potluck in June at the Free School, olympiazines@gmail.com

Pens, Pencils and Photocopiers!—is held in July in London. Live drawing competitions on an overhead projector!
comicsandzines.wordpress.com/

Philly Zine Fest is in Sept
www.phillyzinefest.com

Portland Zine Symposium www.pdxzines.com An annual conference and zine social exploring facets of underground publishing and DIY culture that aims to create greater communication and community between diverse creators of independent media and art. This fun, free and open event helps people promote their work and share skills and information related to zines and zine culture.

PrakalpanA MovemenT in its 40th year, takes place each September in Kolkata, India. All the concerned or discerned writers, poets, critics, artists and people who are or were once associated with this movement, prakalpana@gmail   Vattacharja Chandan, P40 Nandana Park, Kolkata 700034, India. vattacharjachandan.blogspot.com

Richmond Zine Fest features workshops, tabling, etc. www.richmondzinefest.org.

San Francisco Zine Fest Annual event, usually in September. www.sfzinefest.com

San Francisco Anarchist Bookfair is in March in Golden Gate Park.

Small Press and Alternative Comics Expo is in Columbus, OH in April
backporchcomics.com/space.html

Small Press Expo is held in October bringing hundreds of small press artists, publishers, readers, booksellers, and distributors.
spxpo.com

Southern Girls Convention moves from city to city each year and is in its 10th year. It's an annual grassroots meeting for networking, organizing, educating, agitating, and activism, devoted to empowering women, girls, and transfolks in the South, and to furthering the struggle for social justice. SGC is open to everyone, regardless of gender, age, or geographic location.
southerngirlsconvention.org

Staple Austin, TX is in March www.staple-austin.org

Stumptown Comics www.pdxcomix.com

This Is Not Art is Australia's premier independent, emerging, and experimental arts festival held annually in Newcastle, NSW in October. www.thisisnotart.org.

Twin Cities Zine Fest features an art show, craft demonstrations, live music, guest speakers, and panel discussions, plus some of the Midwest's best self-made talent each July. zinefest.org

Vilnius Zine Fest is in Lithuania in May

Zine-a-Polooza This convention and exhibit for DIY publishers held annually in Georgia. www.zine-a-polooza.info

Zine Camp is put on by the IPRC in Portland, OR. Two days per week in the summer of each year for folks 12-17. Camp is geared towards self-expression and empowerment through open access to space, information and materials necessary to create your own projects. Cost of enrollment is $125, with scholarships available.
annmarieomalleya@gmail.com

Zine Meet-Up Sponsored by Meetup.com, this is a site that helps organize monthly gathering of zine editors in any of 545 cities around the world.

online resources

http://zinewiki.com/
http://www.zinebook.com
http://grrrlzines.net/
http://zineplosion.yuku.com/
http://www.photocopyheart.proboards79.com/
http://members.tripod.com/altzines/
http://community.livejournal.com/zine_scene/
http://community.livejournal.com/zinesters/
http://community.livejournal.com/stolensharpie/
http://groups.myspace.com/zinesters
http://groups.yahoo.com/group/zinesters/
http://groups.yahoo.com/group/zinelibrarians/
http://www.blogtalkradio.com/thezineshow

updates for this edition

Most of the serious Amazon reader reviews of the first edition of this book were not complimentary. They complained that:

1)It was too self-referential.

2)It was geared more toward ziners who were willing to invest a bit of money in their publishing efforts.

3)It was inappropriate for kids because of five pages on Bill's specialty—sex zines and queer zines (as if acknowledging the existence of these things was the same as including sexually oriented material).

With that in mind, this edition is vastly updated and entirely rewritten. Someone would be hard pressed to find a sentence that came through unchanged. The sex has been removed, the examples have been broadened, and the breadth of zines that it covers is much bigger.

GO BE MIGHTY.